GIFF W9-AUY-518

WE THOUGHT YOU MIGHT
LIKE THIS

CAPPY

# DOROTHY ELIZABETH

Dorothy Elizabeth

# DOROTHY ELIZABETH

*Building a Traditional
Wooden Schooner*

## Roger F. Duncan

W. W. NORTON & COMPANY
NEW YORK • LONDON

For information about permission to reproduce selections from
this book, write to Permissions, W. W. Norton & Company, Inc.,
500 Fifth Avenue, New York, NY 10110

This book is composed in Janson
Book design and composition by Susan McClellan
Manufacturing by Haddon Craftsmen
Frontispiece: Kathy Bray
Cover photograph: Roger S. Duncan
Cartography: Jacques Chazaud
Illustrations: Marcus Schone

Library of Congress Cataloging-in-Publication Data
Duncan, Roger F.
  Dorothy Elizabeth : building a traditional wooden schooner /
Roger F. Duncan; illustrations by Marcus Schone
      p.    cm.
  Includes index.
  ISBN 0-393-04904-3
  1. Dorothy Elizabeth (Schooner) 2. Schooners – Design and
construction. 3. Ships, Wooden – Design and construction.
I. Title.
VM311.F7D8597 2000
623.8'44--dc21

                                                    00-024565

W. W. Norton & Company, Inc., 500 Fifth Avenue,
New York, NY 10110
www.wwnorton.com

W. W. Norton & Company Ltd., 10 Coptic Street, London,
WC1A 1PU

1  2  3  4  5  6  7  8  9  0

For
Mary Chandler Duncan

# Contents

|  | Preface | 11 |
| I | The Pattern on the Shop Floor | 15 |
| II | "Let's Build the Little Schooner" | 26 |
| III | Why Build a Wooden Boat? | 36 |
| IV | Design | 44 |
| V | Engine | 50 |
| VI | Getting Ready | 59 |
| VII | Getting Started at Last | 67 |
| VIII | Splicing Wire | 76 |
| IX | Bending Frames | 87 |
| X | Planking | 96 |
| XI | The Crash | 112 |
| XII | Back to the Schooner | 116 |
| XIII | *Eastward* | 125 |
| XIV | Homecoming | 135 |
| XV | Summer's Over | 147 |
| XVI | Rate, Time, and Distance | 157 |
| XVII | "How's the Schooner Coming, Cap?" | 164 |
| XVIII | Rigging | 175 |
| XIX | Launching | 182 |
| XX | Under Way | 196 |
| EPILOGUE | Is It Worth It? | 206 |
|  | Glossary | 210 |
|  | *Dorothy Elizabeth*'s lines | 231 |
|  | Time Line | 227 |
|  | Index | 233 |

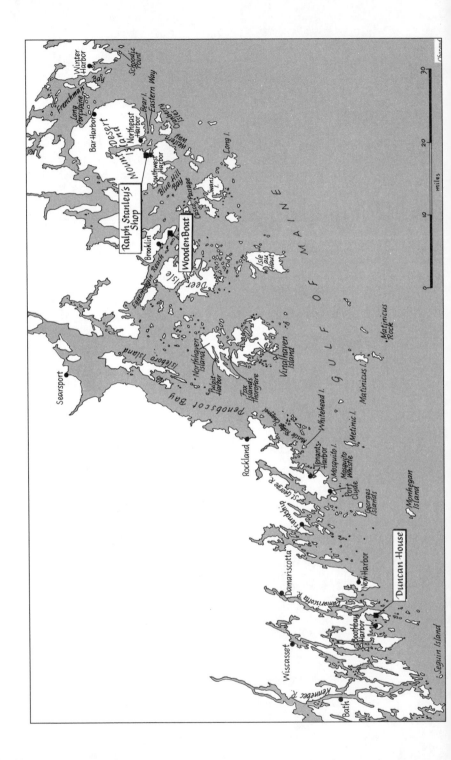

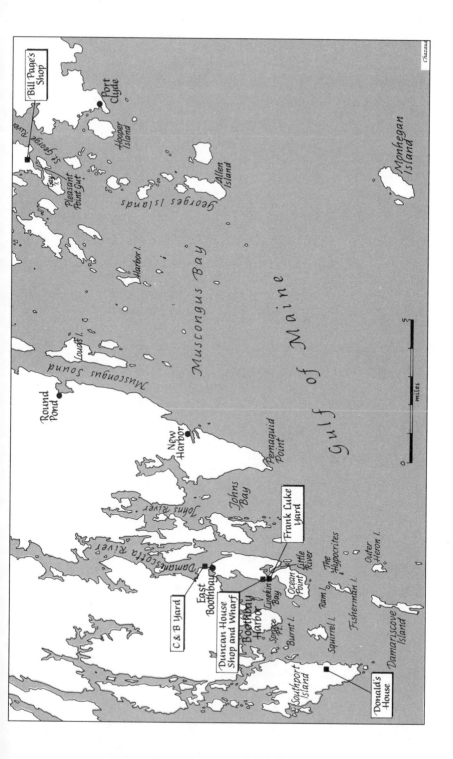

Bill Page's Shop

Port Clyde

Hooper Island

St. George's River

Gay Is.

Pleasant Point Gut

Allen Island

Georges Islands

Harbor I.

Muscongus Bay

Louds I.

Muscongus Sound

Round Pond

New Harbor

Pemaquid Point

Gulf of Maine

Monhegan Island

Johns Bay

Johns River

Damariscotta River

C & B Yard

East Boothbay

Duncan House Shop and Wharf

Boothbay Harbor

Spruce Bay

Burnt I.

Squirrel I.

Frank Cuke Yard

Linekin Bay

Ocean Point

Little River

The Hypocrites

Ram I.

Fisherman I.

Outer Heron I.

Southport Island

Damariscove Island

Donald's House

miles

Chazaud

# PREFACE

THIS IS A BOOK ABOUT HOW MUCH FUN IT IS TO BUILD A schooner. The story encompasses unforeseen distress, frustration, and some disappointment, but it abounds in equally unforeseen good fortune. While much of the pleasure came from the creation of a beautiful vessel, fully as much came from our acquaintance with the people the schooner drew to her, a subject more properly developed in the epilogue.

*Dorothy Elizabeth* is still far from finished. We were so eager to launch her and to sail her before winter that we bypassed other work and went directly to rigging. She needs more ballast. We need a binnacle and chests for cockpit seats. The cabin still lacks a ceiling, lockers, bunks, a galley, and a chart table. We are working on these. However, she sails and she sails well. We ran out of time.

You will notice that there is almost no mention of money in this story. The values here discussed cannot be measured in money. We spent no more than we had to, and we spent it where it counted most. Fortunately, enough was available.

There is perhaps too much of "I" in this book. *Dorothy Elizabeth* is something Mary and I are doing together. Mary has had a part in every decision, sometimes the best part. She sanded, painted, passed the ball for servings. She bent sails and set up rigging. She engineered and hosted two outstanding parties, the Homecoming and the Launching. She was largely responsible for my rapid recovery from the Crash and hustled me when I needed hustling. In many places where I wrote "I," I could have written "we."

ABOUT A YEAR AFTER *Dorothy Elizabeth* was launched, Ralph Stanley, her designer and builder, was awarded a National

Heritage Fellowship by The National Endowment for the Arts. This award was established "to recognize, reward and encourage the highest standards of traditional artistry in the United States."

Our country has recognized Ralph Stanley as an artist in the design and construction of traditional wooden boats. Not only are his boats a delight to the eye, but each is designed for its purpose, be it hauling lobster traps, cruising the Maine coast or racing. Ralph's boats are strongly and beautifully built, each joint and seam a work of art. *Dorothy Elizabeth* stands as one of his best creations. This book should show how this award was so justly earned.

# DOROTHY ELIZABETH

# I

## THE PATTERN ON THE SHOP FLOOR

RALPH STANLEY STARTED TO BUILD OUR SCHOONER WITH a broom. He carefully swept a 14-foot square of white-painted plywood on the shop floor. His son Richard came after him with the powerful Shop-Vac, sucking up every grain of grit and sawdust. Then they laid down on the plywood a 30-inch-wide strip of Mylar, a strong translucent plastic on which were conflicting and confusing blue lines generated by computer. After five strips were laid down and carefully matched, we saw, life size, the shape our boat would actually take. They transferred the lines in the right upper corner to a piece of builder's paper, the pattern from which the stem of the boat would be cut out of heavy gray oak. Our boat was started. It was January 1997.

WHO ARE WE and why are we building a boat? We, Mary and I, are outdoor, mountain, and saltwater people, and teachers by nature and profession. We have sailed our 32-foot Friendship sloop, *Eastward*, for 40 summers from our home in East Boothbay, Maine. We have sailed day parties to pay the boatyard bills. We have cruised from the Saint John River, New Brunswick, to Newport, Rhode Island, and visited most of the harbors between more than once. We have lived aboard for weeks at a time and survived squalls, calm, fog, and some pretty snappy thunderstorms. At 80, I can still hoist the mainsail and still pull the anchor. Mary, at 82, can still set and take in the jib and staysail and step out on the float with a dock line if the Old Man can get her close enough so she doesn't have to leap too far; and she is the only grandmother in Maine who can take in a gaff topsail in a breeze.

But *still*. That word *still* was giving us the shivers. It implied that people didn't expect us to be able to hoist a sail much longer. It said we were over the hill and sliding down the other side. We realized with a chilly shudder that should it come off really rough and dirty, if we had to take a party in a hard reefing breeze, if the anchor dragged at midnight, we would be glad of some muscle aboard. If one of us fell overboard, a strong back would be the difference between an adventure and a disaster.

Where was this leading? Did it mean that soon we would not sail alone? That we would have to solicit a crew? That the family would ask who would keep the incompetent old duffers out of trouble today and find only one reluctant volunteer? Would it come to an agreement that a grandson could use the boat as his own if he would take Grampie and Granny for a sail on a nice day when they wanted to go? On our own boat? *Never.* We were not about to be wrecked on the lee shore of old age. Before that happened, we would sell *Eastward* and buy a boat we could handle ourselves.

But selling *Eastward* was not a popular idea in our family. We had had her built, bare hull, when our twins were 14 and their brother was 11. All five of us had worked together to rig her, to build cockpit seats and nail together bunks, galley, and lockers.

I had spliced in the wire rigging. A boy passed the ball while I swung the serving mallet to finish the splices. For years we had scraped, sanded, and painted together. I installed the first engine, and the second and third. The boys took turns being mate while Mary answered the telephone to sign on parties and beat the bushes—hotels and motels—when business was slow. We cruised together, sailed together, raced together. When grandchildren appeared, they too joined the crew. Brother, sisters, nieces, and nephews shared the boat with us. To sell *Eastward* would leave big holes in many lives.

So what to do? Of our three sons, only Bob, an assistant headmaster, had enough summer vacation to even consider using and maintaining *Eastward*, and he could not afford to maintain her as a yacht. His son Alec, however, aged 18 in the summer of 1996, was enthusiastic about getting his Coast Guard license to carry passengers and running *Eastward* as a party boat. After we laid up *Eastward* in the fall of '96, I signed her over to Bob.

That wasn't easy, but it was the right thing to do, the constructive, creative thing, and we did it.

Now, what kind of a boat would we get? Such a decision is not made hastily. We approached that pattern on the shop floor by an uncertain course.

ONE BRIGHT BLUE AFTERNOON in 1995, Mary, Bob, Alec, and I were beating westward through Casco Passage in Blue Hill Bay with a fine working breeze, *Eastward*'s lee rail just out of water, mainsail, staysail, topsail, and jib full and drawing.

"Ready about. Hard alee. Can't quite fetch that can buoy. Hard alee again." And what a lovely day!

Astern came a low, fast ketch with a bone in her teeth, and she went by us like smoke. She made the can we couldn't, sailed closer to the wind, went faster through the water, and was through the passage and far on her way while we were still short-tacking. There's our new boat!

She was a 28-foot Herreshoff-designed Rozinante ketch, of which there were several on the coast. We found one for sale, *Swift*, and persuaded the owner to let us try her out one quiet foggy day. She sailed like a ghost—slipped quietly through the water, climbed to windward, was responsive and eager. In short, she looked like the answer to prayer.

However, as we continued our cruise toward home in *Eastward*, we found a fresh head wind and a steep chop coming out of Muscle Ridge Channel. *Eastward* jumped into the short seas and banged her way through them, throwing wide fans of spray to leeward. Sitting dry in our big cockpit, we wondered how *Swift* would be making it. Narrow, deep, heavily ballasted with low freeboard, she would have been wet as a half-tide rock. We could see ourselves in oilclothes dodging the top of every wave. We remembered her short tiller just clearing the mizzenmast, the narrow side decks, and the tiny foredeck. Well, we rationalized, we don't have to go out in this kind of weather. But we do, and we will.

In *Eastward*'s cabin that night, warmed by her Shipmate stove, with room for four of us to stretch out or sit at the cabin table for dinner, we thought how it would be aboard *Swift*. Two bunks meeting in a V under the low, narrow foredeck, a tiny stove, no head, no place for water jugs—she had no tank—no place to stow the outboard motor and gasoline tank, no place to stow oilclothes, no place for an icebox. Somehow, we had to do better.

We thought of the Herreshoff H-28, a neat ketch about the same size but more of a boat. Our thoughts turned and twisted, decided and undecided. We wrote to a friend in a broker's office and got a number of unsatisfactory suggestions, and came to no conclusion.

Then, in September, the course toward those lines on the shop floor straightened out, although we couldn't see it at the time.

After we had agreed to give *Eastward* to Bob but while we still owned her, and after Alec had gone back to school, Mary and I cruised down east on a mission to determine how in 1775 the pilot of His Majesty's armed schooner *Halifax* struck a rock south of what is now Halifax Island, east of Roque Island in Englishman Bay. Her commander, Lieutenant Nunn, had been ordered by Admiral Graves in Boston "to move suddenly from place to place without [his] Intentions being previously made known to any person" in the hope of catching or at least discouraging colonial vessels smuggling arms and ammunition. *Halifax*, guided by a local pilot, left Little Cranberry Island near Mount Desert at 3 A.M. headed east for Machias. About noon, with a "fresh gale" from the west-southwest, with the pilot at the tiller, she struck the rock and was lost, although none of her crew was hurt. I wondered whether the pilot was a patriot intent on protecting smugglers, was ignorant, or was careless. The court-martial laid all the blame on him but did not give his name. I wanted to see that rock for myself and try to reconstruct the situation.

We approached the rock on a lovely September day with a west-southwest breeze and saw how the pilot might have been confused. We photographed the scene, landed on the island where the crew camped, and came up with no clear conclusion; but at least we had seen the rock from the pilot's point of view.

On our way back, we sailed into the Eastern Way at Mount Desert in the gathering dark before a growing easterly in a lump of a sea and a drizzle. Off Bear Island, Mary took in the topsail and dropped the mainsail. I started the engine and took in the headsails while she took the wheel and dodged lobster traps. We motored gently into the calm of Northeast Harbor in the almost-dark. There seemed to be no doubt that we were still entirely capable of handling the vessel.

We lay in Northeast Harbor the next day in fog and rain, went ashore for a shower and a lunch, and spent the afternoon dismantling the head, seeking the source of its malaise without success. We reassembled it to its great satisfaction and ate dinner in the lamplight. There seemed no doubt that we could still enjoy cruising even at some of its less delightful moments. We discussed the future, the Rozinante, the H-28, other alternatives.

The next day the fog lay thick over the Western Way and the Mount Desert hills. One of us—the log doesn't say which—suggested, "Let's go over to Southwest Harbor and ask Ralph Stanley what it would cost to build just the ketch we want."

We were getting closer and closer to those lines on the floor, but we still didn't know it.

At his boat shop in Southwest Harbor, Ralph Stanley builds, repairs, and maintains wooden boats. Two winters earlier, he did extensive surgery on *Eastward*—many new frames, some new planks, first aid to the keel—two months' work. We visited the operating room almost every week to observe the procedure and were impressed by the skill, accuracy, and judgment of Ralph and his crew. *And* it is a pleasure to talk with him.

So out we went into the choking-thick fog, found Southwest Harbor, picked up one of Ralph's moorings, and went ashore to his shop to visit.

Ralph welcomed us quietly and enthusiastically. He is quite a tall man, a little stooped, giving the impression of relaxed strength. He was dressed in work clothes: khaki pants and shirt with a sweater against the chill fog.

The shop smelled of cedar. A new cutter, just planked, stood next to the backbone of a small sloop: just stem, keel, and sternpost, horn timber and counter. I could see where the lead keel met the deadwood, but to find the joint where the keel met the stem, I had to scratch with my fingernail. Ralph's son Richard, probably in his late 30s, was on his knees on the floor with a pencil, a pair of dividers, a rule, and a heavy chunk of oak, measuring marks on the white-painted floor. He looked up and greeted us, for he had worked on *Eastward* two winters before. At the bench beside the cutter stood Andrea, a tall, strong lady with long braided hair. She had come from Germany, attended the Washington County Vocational and Technical Institute–Boatbuilding Division at Eastport, married, and settled in Ralph's yard.

We admired the cutter, for you don't rush into these things. We climbed the staging and looked down into her where we could see her whole shape at once.

"Who designed her, Ralph?"

"I did. She is in the English cutter tradition, very narrow and deep."

"Quite different from a Friendship sloop or a lobster boat."

"It's kind of interesting to do something different." We climbed down.

"Ralph, we want to talk boats. We're giving *Eastward* to our son Bob, and we would like to know what it would cost to build a little ketch." Ralph led us outside to the office, which was not big enough for all it contained. I have recollections of a big desk pretty well covered with papers; low bookshelves spilling catalogues, brochures, and who-knows-what; a chair behind the desk and another on the other side. Richard came in with us and found places for all of us to sit. Again I asked Ralph the simple question: "What would it cost to build a ketch about 28 feet, bare hull? Just roughly. Nothing I would want to hold you to." I avoided saying "ball-park figure." I detest the tattered metaphor.

Ralph sat wedged into the corner beyond the desk.

"You know, I don't much like a ketch. I like a schooner a good deal better."

"You built a little schooner once, didn't you?" I asked.

"Yes, and she's for sale now down at Mystic for about $19,000."

"We got a picture of her here somewhere," said Richard, going on his knees in front of the bookcase, shuffling papers.

"What are we waiting for? Let's go to Mystic."

Richard came up with a brochure showing a pretty little black clipper-bowed schooner with a Marconi mainsail and one big jib.

"I suppose we could re-rig the main and make it gaff-headed," I hazarded.

No comment from the corner.

"You know, when you go down her hatch, all you see is a big centerboard."

"Oh, she's shoal draft? What does she draw?"

"She'll sail on a heavy dew."

"My father had a shoal-draft schooner. She was not much to windward in a chop. What's she got for power?"

"Outboard."

That did it. I didn't want her at any price. A cabin divided by a huge centerboard trunk, a Marconi mainsail, slow to windward, and an outboard motor that had to be stowed somewhere and like all outboards spun a small wheel very fast and would not push a vessel against wind and sea.

"Well, Ralph, what would it cost to build a proper schooner 28 feet long? Just give me an idea."

Marion Stanley came in. We had first met her when I was collecting material for a book on Friendship sloops.

We had seen the Stanleys once or twice every year since then, sometimes at Friendship Sloop Society meetings or at symposia of the Maine Maritime Museum. I had read a paper one year on the fishing industry, and Ralph had read one the following year on boatbuilding on Mount Desert, for Ralph is both a historian and a boatbuilder. Marion was always there too, very cheery, always looking ahead. Mary and Marion had shared Friendship Sloop Society meetings and had met at the Society's annual regattas through the years. In 1996 Mary was given the *Chrissy* Award by the Society for being a strong supporter of her family on the water, and the next year it was given to Marion. Besides raising a family of two boys and two girls, she is an accomplished needleworker. When we had visited Southwest Harbor on an earlier cruise that summer, she had come aboard with a square she was knitting for an afghan. Now she blew into the office, bearing in her outstretched arms the completed afghan.

About 4 feet by 5, it suddenly dominated the office. Each 7½-inch square was white with a red rose and green leaves sewed in. Graced by Marion's smiling face over the top of it, it was a burst of ordered color in a scene otherwise drab and confused. She threw it over Mary and said, "For you."

Mary was overwhelmed, sought words to express her surprise and delight. A poet cannot be satisfied with a mere "Thank you."

"You want a self-bailing cockpit?" put in Ralph.

"No, I don't think so. It would have to be so shallow, you would feel you were sitting on top of the boat, not in it. And it would have to be so near the waterline that as soon as she heeled, the water would come up the scuppers."

"Gaff rigged?"

"Yes. On fore and main. I'm kind of used to the gaff rig, and I like the sail to come down when I slack the halyard. That's a real good thing if you have to shorten sail when it's blowing."

"Where were you when Hurricane Edward came through last week?"

"We were hiding in Little River on a big mooring with a big anchor out to windward. It was easterly. Must have been pretty lumpy in here where you're open to the east."

"Kind of rough but not too bad up near the head of the harbor. I had to go to Deer Isle that day, and when I came back and looked out, my lobster boat was gone. Before I went to look for her, someone called to say he had seen her go adrift near high water and blow right down on the ledge. She struck several times and nearly capsized, but went right over the ledge and into deep water on the other side. Someone tied her up at Hinckley's marina. She was scraped up some, but she didn't leak a drop."

23

"She must have been a pretty well built boat," I offered.

"I built her in 1960. You want a clipper bow?"

"No, I don't believe. We've done the Friendship sloop thing." A picture was forming in my mind faster than a computer could have done it. We came to talk ketch, but now I saw a neat little round-bowed schooner.

"I want her round-bowed like a Gloucester fisherman. Ralph, give me some idea of what kind of money we're talking about."

"I got to draw some pictures."

Mary and Marion were talking grandchildren, which distracted me for a while.

"Would you have time to build her this winter?"

"We'd maybe have to hire some more help," put in Richard.

"When we finish the little sloop, we could put her in there," said Ralph. There followed calculations of other projects, repair jobs, and maintenance work, and finally the answer, "Prob'ly. I guess we could find a way."

Observe what happens when two people really want to build a schooner.

"Well, Ralph, I have to know roughly how much money I have to have in the bank."

"I'll have to draw some pictures."

"But I don't want you to do a lot of design work if we can't afford to build her."

"Let me draw some pictures."

It finally soaked in that I wasn't going to get an answer today, that I was asking too much.

"Well, all right. We'll sail home to Boothbay and call you. Then we can drive down and look at the pictures when you're ready."

Mary gathered up the afghan and suggested she leave it with Marion until we came back in the car, lest it get wet or dirty aboard *Eastward* on the trip home. Marion went to get a plastic bag to protect it.

"Don't go to a lot of trouble, Ralph, because we may just be cutting paper dolls. We may not be able to afford it."

"Let me draw some pictures and then you come down and look at them."

Marion came back with the bag. We made our way back aboard, lit the lamps—for it gets dark early on September 10—torched up the stove, and assessed what we had learned:

1. We like a schooner better than a ketch.

2. Ralph could find time and a place to build her.

3. Ralph liked the schooner he had built, but she was not what he would have built for himself.

4. Ralph and Richard wanted to build a proper schooner.

5. There was no one we would rather have do it.

6. Marion and Ralph and their family were people to admire, respect, and treasure.

7. The afghan was a beautiful thing.

# II

## "Let's Build the Little Schooner"

WE SAILED HOME IN TWO DAYS, THE SECOND ON THE back of a building easterly with a darkening sky and a growing sea. We beat up Linekin Bay, rail down, in a cold rain. When Mary picked up our mooring, we ended our last cruise as owners of *Eastward*.

A few days later, Ralph called.

"You better come down. I have a boat I want you to see."

It takes two hours and 40 minutes to drive from our house to Ralph's, and we really pushed right along. He took us to see a 28-foot sloop he had built. She was laid up for the winter in a big shed with a fleet of others. Ralph found a ladder and we climbed aboard, expecting to be delighted. We were not.

She was wide, her width exaggerated by her dark teak deck. The cockpit was self-bailing, too shallow, and too wide to brace your feet across, and it was obstructed by a long, heavy tiller.

We tried to imagine her as a schooner. Here would be the mainmast, there the foremast. She'd need a longer bowsprit. We rebuilt her as we sat there, and still I didn't like her very much. We went below. Of course it was dark because we were in the shed, but even allowing for that, the varnished paneling and cherry-wood trim, although elegant and beautifully crafted, was oppressive. We went back on deck and climbed down the ladder.

We walked all around her. "Chubby" was the word that came to mind.

"Will she sail, Ralph?"

"I've been after him to give her a longer bowsprit and a double head rig. She's for sale."

She seemed wide, heavy, reluctant.

We stood under her fat stern.

"This isn't really what we had in mind, Ralph. We want something light, quick—a vessel that wants to go." Ralph didn't seem to mind our criticism of the boat he built. Indeed, he seemed quite pleased that we were dissatisfied. I came back to the same old question, which now sounded like an echo re-echoed. "What would it cost to build a proper little schooner, bare hull?"

"Well, I think it would take about 1,500 hours."

Standing in that drafty shed under the stern of that sloop, he finally gave us a figure on the sunny side of our bank account. He really wanted to build the boat, and we really wanted him to be the one to do it.

"We might be able to swing it."

On the drive back to Ralph's house: "I wouldn't want you to spend too much on sandpaper. Lobster boat finish is just fine for us. And no varnish at all."

"When we do a lobster boat, after she's planked, we lay her on her side so we don't have to work over our heads and caulk her and pay the seams. Then we lay her on the other side and caulk that and then paint her and launch her. What color do you want to paint her?"

Years ago I asked the same question of Captain Ed McFarland, a New Harbor fisherman and boatbuilder who was largely responsible for my early education. He replied:

"There's only one color for a boat—white. White paint is white lead and oil. It goes into the wood and preserves it and reflects the heat. The bottom is red, the color of copper oxide, which is the important part of copper paint, and the deck is buff. The old-timers made paint from seal oil, skim milk, and ochre from the paint mines, and the paint mines around here were buff."

Ralph laid out on the kitchen table a drawing of a lovely little schooner, gaff rigged on fore and main with a round bow and a single big jib. It took a minute to take her in, but she was breathtaking. I could scarcely speak.

"Now that is just what we had in mind." He showed us the lines, the cross sections, the waterlines and buttock lines. She had the wedge-shaped bow, flaring above the waterline, the slack bilges amidships, a good drag to the keel, and the flat run of the Gloucester schooners and the later Friendship sloops. She would sit lightly on the water, a lovely creation.

We assumed we would be able to build her, although we did not yet have a figure for materials and engine, nor had we estimated what it would cost to finish her from a bare hull. That might be considerable, for "bare hull" means only the outside shell of the boat, planked and decked. In this case, we would ask Ralph to make the spars and install the engine, but the sails, rigging, head, pump, ceiling, and accommodations in the cabin could cost nearly as much as the bare hull, even if we did them ourselves. At least we did not know we could not build her. She already had a life of her own in our minds.

On our way home, we stopped for lunch and raised a glass to our new boat. What is her name?

Naming a boat is serious business. It will be who she is as long as we own her. It will be who she is on the VHF radio. "This is *Unprepared* calling *Slippery Hitch*. Come in, *Slippery Hitch*." To be repeated at 30-second intervals! "This is Camden Marine Operator holding traffic for *Albert's Toy*. Come in on 26 or 84, *Albert's Toy*." Unacceptable.

*sloop*

*yawl*

*catboat*

*ketch*

*schooner*

**Common yacht rigs**

Names of birds or stars are common and often have good associations. Polaris is the constant center of the celestial sphere's rotation. All the other stars move around it. Aldebaran and Arcturus have stately sounds, are bright and easily found in the sky, and are much used for navigation. Mythological names are tempting. Poseidon I would avoid; he gave Odysseus a very hard time on his way home; but Athene, Greek goddess of wisdom, is tempting. Indian names—Penobscot, Muscongus, Monhegan, Matinicus—have attractive connotations. *Eastward* was an inspired name. When she was built, my first inclination was to name her *Mary C. Duncan*. However, she was to be used as a party boat. We would be posting signs, and we were reluctant to plaster the town with Mary's name. So if we were not going to name the boat after her, Mary could choose the name.

When my father owned a cruising boat, we always headed eastward toward Penobscot, Isle au Haut, Mount Desert, Schoodic. Westward lay Boothbay, Portland, and the desolate, harborless beaches beyond. But eastward lay lands of romance and adventure. So *Eastward* she was named. *Eastward II* was impossible. The new boat needed a new name, a name of her own.

My father's two boats, owned successively, had been named *Dorothy* after my mother. Mary's mother's name was Elizabeth. The two slipped together with a click. We raised a glass to *Dorothy Elizabeth*.

ON THE LONG STRAIGHT ROAD from Ellsworth to Bucksport, Mary asked, "How was it we switched so fast from a ketch to a schooner? What is so great about a schooner?"

My first response was "The gods decreed it." But even they must have had a reason.

We had thought of a ketch at first because the Rozinante *Swift* was a ketch. Also, I had been to sea on a ketch, served as a member of the crew of a 38-foot ketch on a voyage from Morehead City, North Carolina, to Saint Thomas, Virgin Islands, in 1983. On the first night out we ran into a northeaster. About dark—the month was November—with a short, steep sea running, the skipper called for a reef in the mainsail. Good call. I found that one can be very seasick indeed and still do what one has to do. I was glad to find that the mainsail lay over the middle of the vessel and that to pass the earing on the end of the boom, I didn't need to hang out over the stern but could stand on the cabinhouse. Later, we found that in sudden squalls we could shorten sail quickly by yanking down the mizzen, easily reached from the cockpit. Surprisingly, it did not upset the balance of the sail plan as one might expect. Furthermore, this cruise in a ketch had been a delightful experience with all kinds of weather, from bare poles to flat calm. After the first night, I had enjoyed every bit of it. We had scarcely thought seriously about a schooner until Ralph brought it up.

I had sailed several schooners coastwise. In 1950, with a crew of green boys, we ran from Cape Ann to the Isles of Shoals before a brisk southwester, winged out, mainsail to port and foresail to starboard, with no great tendency to yaw. A sloop would have tried to turn around as she came down every sea and look us in the eye. I took a party of adults on a 40-foot schooner and found her very handy. By trimming and slacking main and staysail sheets, we could steer her quite accurately, and we set a fine big fisherman staysail between the masts. Her mainsail was bigger than that of the ketch, big enough to have some real authority. With sheets eased a little, sailing about 70 degrees from the wind, she marched along impressively. My father had a 36-foot shoal-draft schooner, *Dorothy*, that we sailed through intricate passages among the ledges and into narrow little gunkholes. When it blew hard, there were various options: reefed main, with foresail and staysail; foresail and staysail; or, in extreme circumstances, reefed foresail. She could be sailed around the harbor under foresail alone or even sailed straight backward by trimming the mainsheet flat amidships and backing foresail or staysail. But I suspect that her real attractions, like those of a good wife, were her family background and her good looks.

*Dorothy Elizabeth* is the direct descendant of those fast, able Gloucester fishing schooners designed by men who were at once artists and engineers, built by superb craftsmen, and sailed by rugged fishermen, some of the ablest seamen who ever stood in boots. Gloucester schooners brought in fresh haddock and halibut from the rich waters east of Georges Bank, one of the world's most furious places in a winter northeaster. These schooners clawed off the shoals against wind and sea and ran before the gale for the Boston market. They seined mackerel in spring and summer from the Virginia Capes to the Gulf of St. Lawrence, harpooned swordfish on Georges in summer, and carried frozen herring from Newfoundland in winter. The Gloucester schooner, like the clipper ship and the Friendship sloop, is an artist's marriage of form and function, and here lies true beauty.

A day or two later we got a figure on materials and engine, took a guess at the expense of materials to finish her from "bare hull," and on September 30 called Ralph Stanley and said, "Let's build the little schooner."

## This is the way Ralph Stanley saw it:

WHEN ROGER AND MARY came to my shop in September of 1996, I was surprised when they announced that they were giving up *Eastward*, but I could understand their wanting a boat that was easier to handle. For myself, at 67 years of age, sails did not hoist as easily as when I was 35, and I knew Roger was older than I.

They mentioned a new boat 28 feet in length with a ketch rig. I have always liked a ketch rig but on a much larger boat. The mizzenmast on a 28-footer would always be in the way, and there is no chance to have deck travelers for the main- and mizzen-sheets. On the Rozinante ketch, sails trim directly from the center of the boat, and consequently the boom lifts, allowing the sails to belly out too much for my satisfaction. A traveler allows the boom to be trimmed at the proper angle to leeward while pulling the sail down flatter, making it a more efficient air foil.

Somehow I couldn't see Roger and Mary sailing a ketch. I had known them for some time from attending the Friendship Sloop Regatta at Friendship, Maine. Even before that I had known Roger from reading the *Cruising Guide to the New England*

*Coast* back in the late 1940s and early 1950s, when I sailed on the schooner *Niliraga* out of Northeast Harbor. Also I followed the news articles in the old *Maine Coast Fisherman* about Roger having *Eastward* built, and I knew he was a traditionalist. What could be more traditional than a schooner? They wanted a big, deep cockpit, and decks wide enough to walk forward on. This fitted the 28-foot schooner perfectly, which is deep enough to have the engine completely under the cockpit sole. With 1,500 pounds of lead outside in the keel and enough inside ballast under the cabin sole to trim her to her waterline, she should have an easy motion.

Boats with all their ballast outside and down low tend to have a quick, snappy motion. Those who work in boats prefer an easy motion. A boat with some of the ballast inside may roll deeper but with a slower motion and not take you off your feet, as does a boat with outside ballast down low, which causes the boat to snap upright.

The sails on a schooner are small enough to be easy to handle, and with various combinations can be adjusted to suit whatever conditions wind and wave have to offer. Schooners have been used on the Maine coast for many years, and the virtues of the rig are well known. A man from Vinalhaven who went fishing on schooners out of Portland once told me that he would often see larger beam trawlers when out fishing and thought he would like to get a berth on one. He eventually did, and it was in winter on the Grand Banks. Everything went fine until it came off a gale of wind so they couldn't fish. It got worse and colder, and the steel vessel started to ice up. They lost their heat, their bunks were wet, everything was covered with frost, and they had no hot food. They could keep only enough headway to keep the vessel head to the wind and sea. They were pretty miserable, not being able to sit or lie in their bunks, just stand up and hang onto something solid so as not to be thrown around.

They took an awful pounding. At the worst of it, he looked out and saw several fishing schooners under double-reefed foresails with jumbos riding like ducks. He said he could picture those fellows in the fo'c's'les, all warm and snug, sitting around the tables and riding so easy their teacups wouldn't even upset. He would have given anything to be aboard one of those little schooners. Finally they had to steam off into the Gulf Stream, where the water was warmer, to melt the ice and put the vessel in order.

Designing a boat is a lesson in compromise. You have to balance one desirable feature against another and try to have the right hull shape, rig, and arrangement of usable space to make a comfortable, workable, and seaworthy boat and one that will look right. One disadvantage to the schooner rig is that you have to crawl out onto the bowsprit to furl the jibs. The ketch rig wouldn't need a bowsprit. To rig a schooner without a bowsprit requires a long overhanging bow, and to keep the overall length to 28 feet on deck would mean a shorter waterline length and consequently a lot less room in the boat. Designers of fishing schooners faced the problem of the long bowsprit—many fishermen were washed away to their deaths—by lengthening the boat with the overhanging bow and the jibs all inboard. Many of these schooners were subsequently found to need a short bowsprit after all. These vessels, although longer on deck, had no more capacity than a shorter vessel with a conventional bowsprit. Also, the boat being longer increased the cost to build it.

To get the desired room in the boat, I found I needed the bowsprit but not nearly as long as *Eastward*'s. I tried designing the rig with a single jib, but I couldn't make it balance. Besides, it didn't look right. Double headsails might be a little more work, but they would be smaller and easier to handle individually and could be made to balance the rig much better. Of course a roller furler on the outer jib would solve the problem of getting out on the bowsprit.

It went without saying that Roger and Mary wanted a boat that looked right. One time when I was sailing the *Niliraga*, a 43-foot John Alden–designed centerboard schooner with a double headsail rig and a Marconi main, I was asked to take Miss Mary C. Wheelright and a friend, both elderly ladies, on a cruise. Miss Wheelright brought her hired captain along to help, as I was sailing *Niliraga* all alone. We were sailing to the westward through the Fox Island Thorofare when we met several particularly ugly looking boats sailing east. We made no comments, but the last one was really ugly, and Miss Wheelright's captain said, "My God, the more they come, the worse they look." Those boats just didn't look right.

There is an old saying that if it looks right, it is right, and there is a lot to that. There is no question that a schooner looks right, and over the years it has been proven. Here is a boat that could sail off comfortably to Monhegan and back, or lie in any harbor on the Maine coast and look as if it belonged there.

As to the type of construction and the material for construction, there really was never a question. Carvel planking of Maine cedar on steam-bent Maine oak frames and keel, fastened with silicon bronze, has been proven in Maine-built lobster boats for years. Maine cedar may have a lot of knots, but I think that makes it a tougher wood. Fastening the plank to the frames with silicon bronze screws makes good sense, as after 25 years some deterioration may take place. The screws can be replaced with a size larger. My lobster boats have stood up very well over time, and some have had some hard use. Lobster boat construction was the word for this schooner; good, solid, practical construction— and don't waste a lot of time with sand-paper.

# III

## W H Y   B U I L D
## A   W O O D E N   B O A T ?

A<small>S I WRITE THE FIRST CHECK FOR</small> D<small>OROTHY</small> E<small>LIZABETH</small>, on October 3, 1996, and we find ourselves committed, I ask myself how I can justify spending five-figure money on a toy while so many people are crying out for help. Are there ways in which *Dorothy Elizabeth* can be more than a toy, can be a valued and cherished addition to our coastal community?

What will our money do if we don't build this boat? Right now it is sitting in the bank at a very low rate of interest, an umbrella against a disaster or a rainy day. But that day may never come. Or if it does, we may find a way to deal with it at the time. Why cower under an umbrella when there is no cloud in the sky, lest it rain tomorrow? Better to take a chance and put the money to work where it will be spent over and over again by a great many people.

Let us speculate on what happens to this check I am about to write, and to the others that will follow it. Most of these will be made out to Ralph W. Stanley, Inc. Ralph's daughter, working in the office behind the shop, will deposit it in the bank and pay some of it to herself for her own contribution to building the schooner. Some will go to Richard, who right now is fitting the stem to the heavy oak keel—fitting it so precisely that when the bolts take up the strain, the seam will be watertight and scarcely visible. He has developed this skill over a period of years, a skill that will be lost to the community if he and a few others are not paid to practice it. The others working in the shop have their skills and their shares of the money, and each dispenses it to grocery stores, gasoline stations, tax collectors, banks, charities, and perhaps to a bit of riotous living, thus contributing to the financial support of the entire community.

Some of the money is spent for tools and materials. It would be tedious to trace the course of these dollars back through dealers, truckers, machinists, miners, through loggers and sawyers; but surely these dollars contribute to our total economy.

Finally, Ralph keeps some of this money for his own contribution. He started Ralph Stanley, Inc., and without him it could not exist. Not only does he set a lofty standard of ship carpentry himself, but he tells each person in the shop what to do when, and it is through him and the shop's reputation for good work that people come to him for yachts and lobster boats. These help other people to make a living, and thus the shop is an asset to the community.

However, the existence of a shop building good wooden boats is surely more than an economic asset to a town. People who build wooden boats have unique skills. Almost nothing is square or level about a boat. One needs a flexibility of mind as great as the variety of three-dimensional curves and bevels. Wood itself is not a uniform product extruded from a chemical plant but grows in a forest with all the twists, knots, and knees the flesh is heir to. If you have a boat shop in town, you can see a crew steaming and bending stout oak frames into a vessel, clamping and fastening them, timbering out a whole boat in a day. It is a lesson in coordinated skills. You can watch the process of shaping a flat plank so it will fit a surface in three dimensions, both bent and twisted, and look as natural as clapboards on a house.

When a wooden boat is launched, there is, quite appropriately, a community celebration. When she lies at the wharf or the marina, people stroll idly by the production boats but gather around the wooden boat. She is conspicuous on her mooring and recognizable from as far away as she can be seen at sea. To any community, an active boat shop is a source of pride, a pride that lifts and supports the pride of other people, whatever their skills.

SOME OF THE THINGS we really need to know can be learned aboard a small boat. How many times have I seen a helmsman, trying to get to windward of a buoy, cramp in on the mainsheet and crowd the vessel closer and closer to the wind so the luff of the mainsail is all ashiver, trying by sheer guts and determination to get up to that buoy. And he doesn't make it—ever. The effort is a universal failure, for the sails are starved for wind; forward progress is reduced and leeway increased. Better, as the old-timer said, "to give her a mouthful," sail fast to leeward of the buoy, and take a quick tack.

How often have I seen a courageous skipper carry on in too heavy a breeze. The vessel is heeled over, her lee deck under water and the wind blowing off the top of her sail, his passengers dodging cold spray hurled aft from the weather bow. The vessel is pressed down and driving bodily to leeward. Lots of splash and not much progress. Better to reef, sail more efficiently and comfortably with the vessel dressed properly for the occasion. Thus one soon learns to accept the limitations of the situation and adopt the most reasonable solution—to trim our sails to the wind that blows.

Should the fog shut down, reducing the visible world to a circle 200 feet in diameter, he who has learned his lesson knows that the islands and ledges are just where they have always been, where the chart says they are. The compass points north. The clock ticks on with its accustomed regularity. Rate of speed multiplied by time still equals distance. No panic. He lets arithmetic bring him safe to his mooring. We live in an orderly universe where, if we act in harmony with that order, all may yet be well.

But occasionally the unforeseen assails us. The knot slips. The line parts. The engine chokes and dies. The anchor fouls. Fire! Breakers! Man overboard! Everything happens at once. He who has learned that man's knowledge is incomplete and his vision limited will be prepared for the unexpected.

BESIDES BEING A SOURCE OF WISDOM, *Dorothy Elizabeth* will have a therapeutic value. Consider the healthful effect of contemplating Boothbay Harbor from 5 miles offshore on a pleasant summer day. Roads have become invisible. Gifte shoppes, B&Bs, olde—anything—have vanished. You may see the sparkle of a windshield in the parking lot at Pemaquid Point ("Please pay the attendant."), which is just sufficient to emphasize your complete detachment from it. You may be able to pick out the green stand-pipe on the highest hill, the white dot of Burnt Island Light, the distant gable end of Sample's shipyard, the church spire; but these are landmarks to the essential material, economic, and spiritual life of the community. The trivial—the yacht club, cottages, motels—dissolves in the haze.

Stand 10 or 15 miles farther offshore. You see the Camden Hills. Maybe on a clear day you will see Mount Washington. You see the outlines of islands against the shore, perhaps the faint yellow line of Pemaquid Beach or Reid State Park. You see the coast as Bartholomew Gosnold, George Weymouth, and Captain John Smith saw it—a new, fresh continent, unsmirched. Washington, D.C., is completely invisible.

This far from shore, there is a trace of menace in the scene. You are in deep deep water and help is far away. You have nothing but an inch of cedar between you and a very hostile environment. Dreadful things can happen. The fog can shut down. The wind can breeze up hard and dead ahead, build up a short, steep sea, and keep you out all night. A thunder squall can build up over the land and charge out to sea at you. Under that arching black cloud you feel like the nail waiting for the hammer. But with these things we are prepared to cope. We can find our way in the fog. We can reef and get home in the dark or tomorrow if necessary. We know that thunder squalls are natural expressions of atmospheric physics and bear us no personal malice. These things pass unless we are incredibly unlucky. That possibility, that shadow of danger, perversely adds to the exaltation. Whatever happens, it will be part of the Grand Scheme, the inevitable impersonal march of natural forces. It will not be because some other human wants something we have. It will not be a machination of a man-made government. It will not smell bad, come with the blare of a horn, the screech of rubber. There will be no 6 percent sales tax. The confidence that we can probably meet what comes with our own skill, energy, and God-given wit refreshes the mind and restores the soul.

WE HAVE A PHOTOGRAPH, taken January 10, 1997, of Mary sitting on a pile of cedar boards that will become planks in our schooner. One may regret the destruction of sound, beautiful trees, but they will be transmuted into a new creation of beauty, a new work of art.

Among works of art, a wooden boat is unique. Like a painting, a sculpture, a piece of fine furniture, or even a house, it starts with the creative imagination of the artist and is finished with polished technical skills, often of many people in different trades. A wooden boat is that and more. Beyond being that, it has a purpose that limits the designer. Whether built to carry tea from China, fish from Georges Bank, lobsters from inshore ledges, or, as a yacht, to cross oceans, to cruise comfortably from harbor to harbor, or to go fast, every boat must serve its purpose.

Furthermore, it must be planned and constructed to last for years under stress. Every plank and frame and fastening must do its part in a complicated pattern of tensions and stresses. Even the caulking between the planks serves to stiffen the structure of the entire hull. A wooden boat, sail or power, driven hard into a head sea endures strains that would tear apart a piece of furniture or even a house. People trust their lives to a wooden boat on an ocean that has seldom been called friendly and is sometimes downright hostile. Many a well-built wooden boat has withstood a frightful hammering at sea or on a lee shore and sailed again.

And on top of all this, she must be good looking, for who wants an ugly boat!

WHAT IS BEAUTY GOOD FOR? Beauty is not good *for* anything. It is good in itself. Philosopher and poet Philip Booth writes: ". . . every poem, every work of art, everything that is well done, generously given . . . makes the world more habitable." And surely this applies to our coastal community.

### Ralph Stanley adds:

I CANNOT REMEMBER a time in Southwest Harbor when a boat was not under construction. Even during the early '30s, through the Depression, boats were being built. During the late '20s and early '30s some of the boats under construction may have been rum runners. Many were lobster boats and some were pleasure boats. In the community, boatbuilders were looked up to as special people, along with house builders, but boatbuilders were a cut above. It was a mystery to most people how a boatbuilder could shape, fit, and bend wood and fasten it together in the form of a boat that would not leak and would withstand the rigors of the sea.

There is a difference between a house and a boat. The house

is generally built and stays in one place. The boat is built to move from one place to another and seems to have life. Two identical boats built as near alike as the builder can do it will have distinct characteristics. One boat will handle a little different from the other. The way a boat will handle and ride in the sea will make the boat seem a living thing. Sails or motor will give the boat power to move and be manageable, but sometimes a boat will be unmanageable, as though the boat had a will of its own.

In his poem "The Building of the Ship," Longfellow expresses the notion of a vessel having life with these lines about the launching of the ship:

> And see! she stirs!
> She starts,—she moves—she seems to feel
> The thrill of life along her keel,
> And, spurning with her foot the ground,
> With one exulting joyous bound,
> She leaps into the ocean's arms!

I started to build my first boat, a 28-foot lobster boat, in 1950. I set the boat up in a shop in back of my grandmother's house just outside the center of town. Neighbors and townspeople came to visit and see what I was doing, and they encouraged me to keep with the project. They loaned me tools they knew I needed. In those days everyone in town worked unless they were old or disabled, but even they had worked during their life. They appreciated seeing a young person working, especially building a boat. It took me two winters to build that boat, and when I was finished I thought I would never have the courage to build another. When some person came along soon after, wanting a boat, I couldn't wait to get started. I built many more boats in that old shop.

Times have changed. Today, I think the zoning laws would

not allow a boat to be built in that shop. Those old folks who encouraged me to build a boat are gone, and it seems that now many people have a different attitude. A young person today wanting to build a wooden boat would be hard pressed to find a place to do it. I was lucky to have built my present shop in 1974. Restrictions would not allow me to build there today. It almost seems that some folks view building a wooden boat as a waste of time. I have had inquiries from potential customers about wooden boats, thinking they should be less expensive because a boat built of wood is somehow inferior.

At one point in my life I had thought about making a fiberglass mold and producing fiberglass hulls. I gave it serious thought and concluded that I had spent a good part of my life acquiring the skill and learning how to build with wood. I had perfected my models and construction methods and I thought, "Why should I throw it all away?" If I built a fiberglass mold, I would be stuck with that particular model, as it would be too costly to change the mold. If I built a fiberglass hull, I would lose my interest in building another because I could not change it. I would have built that boat once, and I would have no desire to build that same boat again. When I build a wooden boat, I always see something either in the construction or the model I might change in the next one.

Wooden boats have been built for thousands of years, each builder making improvements from boat to boat in the same way. To me it is a challenge to build each new boat a little better than the one before. Perhaps Longfellow touched on this when he wrote "The Building of the Ship":

Build me straight, O worthy master
Staunch and strong, a goodly vessel,
That shall laugh at all disaster,
And with wave and whirlwind wrestle.

# IV

## DESIGN

"LET'S BUILD THE LITTLE SCHOONER," I HAD SAID TO Ralph on the telephone on September 30. That was all the contract we had. We really did not need any more. We had the lines and sail plan. We had agreed on materials—gray oak and Maine cedar with bronze fastenings—finished fisherman style. We had discussed about how much Ralph should do and at what point in the construction I should take over. And we had agreed that I would make frequent visits to the yard and be in communication by mail and telephone. I asked Ralph if he needed money to get started. He said, "If I need money, I will ask for it." Indeed he did. I got monthly bills for time and materials, neatly and scrupulously drawn up by his daughter Nadine. Most important of all, I knew from his work on *Eastward* the previous winter, from other examples of his work, and from his reputation as the best wooden boat builder in Maine that I could trust him to do a better job than anything I could describe on paper. He trusted me to pay for it. We went to work to build the schooner.

However, we were not building the schooner in a vacuum but in the context of all our other commitments. Ralph and his crew had the cutter and the sloop to finish and, as the summer wound down, boats to haul and store for the winter. He could not sharpen his saw and tear into building *Dorothy Elizabeth*, although he certainly did not forget her.

Nor did we forget her. At home in East Boothbay our telephone chirped with people who wanted to go sailing. One brisk afternoon we took out a very active cardiologist and his father from California. It was blowing about 20 knots and rough. No topsail. Where the southwest wind got a long fetch all the way from Cape Cod, *Eastward* laid her rail in the water, slammed into the steep chop, and threw spray over her shoulder at us. This bothered our passengers not a bit, but no one likes to get wet, so we worked into the smooth water among the islands and ledges. Mary, besides being an excellent foredeck hand, is a gifted conversationalist. Once she had loosened the bung, our cardiologist flowed freely. He flew a glider, a sailplane with long, narrow wings, soaring among the hills of California. He bestrode a windsurfer. He had raced sailboats and iceboats. He wasn't a blowhard. He really had done it. He sailed *Eastward* home quite competently until at the last we took over and showed him how to sail up to a float in a breeze of wind so neatly that Mary had merely to step off with the bow line and take a turn. And we get paid for that!

On several other days, gentle Indian summer days, we took *Eastward* out ourselves, sailing not far, for the sun set early and the twilight was chilly. In October the light is not summer light. The afternoon sun is lower, and its path on the sea is not silver but pewter. As it slides down the sky, the light on the rocks, the spruce trees, the red and yellow maples, is a soft golden light. The low beam throws the black shadow of the mainsail along the shore as we slide up to our mooring.

At the same time I was rowing a single shell 6 miles a day to get in shape for the Head of the Charles Regatta scheduled for October 20 in Cambridge, Massachusetts. It includes an event for people over 60. I had rowed in that event for many years, won medals for being the fastest over 70, and was not about to let this chance go by.

While these events and others were besetting us, we were thinking about that drawing of *Dorothy Elizabeth*. We had no drawing, but I remembered her as a round-bowed gaff-headed schooner with a single big jib set on a boom. As I thought of her, she seemed a bit dumpy. What she needed was a main topsail. Not only would it make her look better, but we knew from our experience with *Eastward* that in light and moderate airs a topsail is as good as an engine. It catches the upper air and often fills when the mainsail hangs slack. Of course it would increase the cost and the labor of making the rigging, and it would be another sail to handle, but it would be small, and Mary handles *Eastward*'s bigger topsail with no great difficulty.

Then I got to thinking about that big single jib on the end of the bowsprit. It was too big for easy maneuvering in harbors and narrow places. Should it come on to blow, the vessel would balance well neither with it nor without it. The prospect of sitting with my knees locked under the end of the bowsprit trying to pass a tack earing to reef the beast while being dunked in cold salt water was not at all attractive. A double head rig with a jib that could be doused with a downhaul from the deck and a staysail set inboard would be much easier on both skipper and mate.

We didn't write or call Ralph about these thoughts. We just thought about them.

On October 9 we had a northeast gale of wind and rain. We ran a line from *Eastward*'s mooring to our guest mooring for belt and suspenders. It blew up to about 40 knots in the hard puffs, rained straight out, and raised an ugly breaking chop. *Eastward* reared back on her mooring line, and the next sea hit her before she could dip into the trough and recover. It was a violent experience, but the gear held.

While all this was going on, there was desk work, housework, firewood to lug, storm windows to wash and hang. Our neighbor John Luke brought in a prefabricated house in four sections, the assembly of which with a crane was too good a show to miss. But I kept thinking about that double head rig and main topsail.

Friday, October 11, the day before the Columbus Day week-end, came in with a strong northwest wind, bright sky, and cool temperature. Because we were closing in on the Head of the Charles, I determined to row in spite of the wind. On West Harbor Pond, Mary helped me launch my 26-foot shell, only 11 inches wide, built of ⅜₂ plywood and weighing about 40 pounds. Mary is my coach and advisor in this project, as in most others. Out of the shelter of the cove, on the long, narrow pond, the high banks offered some protection from the wind. The water was smooth enough and I soon warmed up. The shell sizzled through the water on the fast pieces and glided on the slow ones, the oar puddles kicking up miniature breakers and the scar of the wake fading quickly. The usual flock of gulls flew up, except for two insolent black-backs that sat boldly on the water saying, "Suckers fly."

After shower and lunch the same day, I loaded the bicycle into the car, drove to the C&B boatyard, left the car, rode home, and set sail. The wind, now moderated, gave us a fine boost down the bay and around Ocean Point. When we hardened up for the beat up the river to the yard, we found that we could almost fetch. The wind was working westerly, however, and every time *Eastward* bent to a hard puff and sailed out from under it, she gained yards to windward. We found we could close reach through that blue and gold afternoon almost to the yard. Then it was douse sail, motor into a slip, and our last sail as own-ers of *Eastward* was over.

In the succeeding days we laid up *Eastward* with the help of our son Bob, who is to be her new owner, and his sons Roger and Alec. By Sunday night of the Columbus Day weekend, everything that would move was ashore; the mast, spars, and bowsprit were on a rack at the yard; standing rigging and running rigging was coiled down, labeled, and hung on nails in the garage; sails were bagged and hung up; and the engine was pumped full of antifreeze. *Eastward* lay in a slip with a cover over her cockpit. She would be afloat until cold weather and then be hauled and stored in a shed for the winter. We were ready for *Dorothy Elizabeth*.

The next week focused on the Head of the Charles. After hard 6-mile workouts on the pond on Monday, Tuesday, and Wednesday, I felt as strong as I could be and ready to face the competition. We drove to Cambridge on Thursday with the shell on top of the car and rowed on the Charles on Friday and Saturday. This was exciting, as many crews from all over the country were on the water, going over the course with singles and doubles dodging among them.

The weather was deteriorating, however, and by Saturday night it was raining and blowing hard. On Sunday it blew a living gale. For two eight-oared feather-light shells, each more than 60 feet long, to thread the arches of a stone bridge with a shrieking 50-knot crosswind was sure disaster. The course was declared unrowable, and the regatta was called off. Several thousand disappointed "oarspersons" headed for home, we among the rest, with the rain slamming against the car windows and our light shell lashed on top, shuddering at every heavy gust. That wound up the rowing season for sure.

Then on Tuesday, October 22, we hurried down to Southwest Harbor to see how Ralph was coming on. He unrolled a new plan, saying he had been thinking about the first one and concluded she would be a lot better with a main topsail and a double head rig. We were all delighted, for the new drawing was just what had been growing in my mind for a month. Also he had flattened out the sheer a little forward. Her dumpy look was gone; she was regal.

Next we got down to important details. Ralph would build her "bare hull," which would include deck, house with pine sides and canvas laid over the top, and a fore hatch. She would be steered with a wheel in order to avoid a long tiller that would sweep across the cockpit.

We discussed at length the proper engine. The Universal Atomic 4 gasoline engine we have in *Eastward* has done well for 20 years with the replacement of various parts, but with the whole machine below the waterline, it has been necessary to open the hatch in the middle of the cockpit and descend into the depths below to open or close certain valves whenever the engine was stopped or started. We could avoid this with a freshwater cooling system. Also, the use of a fuel much less likely to explode than gasoline was attractive. After exploring possibilities of various secondhand engines, we finally decided, tentatively, on a 3-cylinder Yanmar diesel, following our principle that we would spend money on what was important and save on all else. Ralph would build the engine beds and install the engine, shaft, stuffing box, stern bearing, and a solid two-bladed propeller. Thus we could be sure that shaft and engine were properly lined up. I have spent too much time in *Eastward*'s bilge, lining up her engine with pry bar, shims, and feeler gauge.

Ralph would also install chainplates because these are not simply bolted to the planks, but each is backed up inside with a false frame notched into the deck clamp to spread the strain throughout the structure of the vessel.

The standing rigging, which I would provide, would be 5⁄16 stainless steel wire. Ralph thought ¼-inch would be enough and probably it would, but ¼-inch seemed very light to me, yet the 3⁄8 we used in *Eastward* was certainly too heavy for *Dorothy Elizabeth*. So without calculating breaking strengths, we decided on 5⁄16 for the lower rigging and ¼ inch for topmast rigging.

Nat Wilson of East Boothbay would make the sails. John Luke, my neighbor, would do the spar ironwork. The hull and spars would be delivered to East Boothbay in the spring by trailer, where I would finish her out and rig and launch her. She would be the prettiest vessel ever to float on Linekin Bay.

# V

## ENGINE

"WHAT'S SHE GOT FOR POWER?" IS ONE OF THE FIRST
questions asked about a new boat. It was a matter to
be settled early in the construction of *Dorothy Elizabeth*.

An engine in a sailing vessel is tucked away in the bilge, the
dampest and dirtiest place aboard, untouched for the most part,
denigrated in conversation, and called upon reluctantly. Then it
is expected to spring into life with all the enthusiasm of its 30
horses.

We are building a sailing vessel. We devote much time to
deciding on the rig, and we enjoy every moment of it. Spars,
sails, wire, and rope; blocks, shackles, deadeyes, and belaying
pins—their pros and cons, their sizes and shapes, we discuss with
pleasure. The decisions made, we write checks with abandon.
Whether gaff or Marconi rig is a serious matter. Whether gasoline or diesel shall be the fuel is dealt with briefly, the decision
made on insufficient evidence, and the check written as reluctantly as we turn the switch.

As boys, learning to handle sloops built on the fisherman
model, we regarded starting the engine as a disgrace, a failure.
Any real sailor should be able to do it under sail. My ally Cap
Williams didn't even have an engine in his boat. Here is a verse
he wrote about one who did—to be sung derisively to the tune
of "Casey Jones."

R. F. Duncan was a sailor man,
Armed with a wrench and a big oil can.
"Steamboat Bill" was his apt nickname;
With a Kermath 8-10 he churned to fame.

The numbers on her bow to the world doth proclaim
That *Dot* and the *Samhar* are one and the same.
The greatest exultation in the summer he doth feel
Is to hear the steady chunking of that little brass wheel.

*Dorothy* was the name of the protagonist's sloop,
*Samhar* a local motor yacht, deeply scorned.

Later, when I started sailing cruising parties of boys, I insisted that we do everything possible under sail. Coming into
Southwest Harbor, on the shores of which dwelt several of my
highly critical friends, we wanted to make a smart impression. I
stationed Bill and Joe on the foredeck to handle halyards and
anchor, and kept Henry aft with me to handle sheets. As we came
up the Western Way before we entered the harbor, I explained
the procedure carefully: First, let go jibsheets and get the jib
down, with Joe to slack the halyard and Bill to take in on the
downhaul. Then, as we approached our berth, Joe was to drop
the staysail. As we shot into the wind, Henry was to trim the
mainsheet. As we lost way, Joe would drop the mainsail, and
when I gave the word, Bill would let go the anchor. All set?
Everyone understood. Lovely afternoon. Nice working breeze.
Anchor hanging from the bowsprit. All in order.

"Down jib." Joe let go the staysail halyard. Bill hauled in on
the jib downhaul, of course to no effect.

"*Jib*, not staysail," I shouted. Confused, Joe hauled the staysail up not all the way and made the halyard more or less fast on
the pin, then let go the jib halyard. Bill had abandoned the
downhaul, which now trailed from the end of the bowsprit. The

jib sagged but didn't come down. Hoping to save a lost situation, I called, "Down staysail," and put her in the wind. Joe let go the staysail halyard, but it lay in a heap on deck where he had dropped it and flew up the mast in a tangle, quite out of reach. Bill, now badly confused with the staysail flapping about his ears, remembering he was to drop the anchor, let it go. It fouled in the downhaul, leaving us with two thoroughly confused boys in a tangle of line on the foredeck, two headsails bagging out to lee-ward, a full mainsail, and the anchor dragging underfoot from the end of the bowsprit.

We dropped the mainsail, let the baggy headsails take us out of the harbor before the wind, manhandled the anchor aboard. I shinned up the mast for the staysail halyard. We straightened out, coiled down, reset our sails, and tried it again with much greater success. None of us would have learned much had we motored in.

Still later, when we began sailing day parties with our sons as crew, we made a point of sailing alongside floats to pick up our passengers. It was good business. If we motored alongside, people watching on the shore, who saw us only in harbor, would say, "Don't go with him. He runs the engine all the time." But when we sailed up to the float, people were impressed with our "unusually skillful seamanship." One man was so impressed that he had to photograph our approach. Our lofty rig soon filled his viewfinder, and he had to step back . . . and back . . . and right overboard.

More than its being good business, there is a satisfaction in calculating, or guessing correctly, the speed of the boat, the effects of wind, sea, and tide, so the mate need only step gracefully onto the float and take a turn with the bow line. It does not always happen that way. We have come too fast and skinned the mate's hands. Once, when we came much too fast and had to swing off and try again, a passenger exclaimed with enthusiastic approval:

"When I come in too fast, I always swing off and come around again."

"What kind of boat do you have?"

"I'm a commercial airline pilot."

Sometimes we come too slowly. We fail to back the staysail in time, she falls off the wrong way, and we go on the rocks. This very seldom happens, but once when it did, our single passenger insisted on going uptown for lobster rolls and beer for the three of us and refused to leave until the tide came in enough to float us off. But for the most part we are successful in sailing alongside. We enjoy it; our passengers enjoy it; our grandson Alec, nourished in the same tradition, enjoys it today.

So insisting on using the wind, either in harbor or at sea, became a habit. If there was a breeze, we used it. Mary and I came out of Muscle Ridge Channel by Whitehead Light about four o'clock on a gloomy September afternoon in 1991, with fog hanging offshore and clouds drooping low. A chilly breeze out of the south blew over miles of cold salt water. However, the wind was far enough to the south so we could fetch Mosquito Bell, 6 miles away on a west-southwest course and a big jump on the way home. We decided to go for it rather than duck into Seal Harbor behind us, or Tenants Harbor to leeward, and face a long beat in the morning. We never even thought of starting the engine.

We sloshed across a gray sea under a gray sky, steering a compass course for a buoy we couldn't see. After about an hour, we heard Mosquito Whistle moaning abeam, and the loom of the land showed on our starboard bow. Then there was Mosquito Bell, more or less ahead. We rounded it, eased sheets, and ran into Port Clyde as the murky day shut down into a rainy night. We picked up a mooring, under sail of course, and called it a day. The Shipmate stove, lamplight, and a hot dinner never felt better. The next morning, Dodge Morgan, who had circumnavigated the world at dizzying speed under sail and the night before had been cowering in his cabin, told me, with respect, that we had looked like something out of the last century.

Of course we love the exhilaration of a beam reach on a fair warm day with the rail just out of the suds and a rainbow under the lee bow, but it isn't all fair winds. We have raced the buoys in Casco Passage, sailing in light airs against the tide—and lost. By working the eddies around the ledges, we contrived to get through; but by that time the tide had turned anyway. It beat motoring.

In the fog, sailing is the way to go. One can hear the surf washing on the shore, the gulls crying on the ledges, and the crows in the trees. The distant bell, the faint moan of a whistle buoy, are most welcome sounds. One morning, beating around Cape Rosier in the fog, the slam of a screen door and the talk of ladies in the kitchen told us it was time to tack. My uncle, skirting Cape Ann in my father's sloop, heard through the fog,

"Hey, this is private property. Get to hell out of here." Under power, you miss these treasured memories.

But what if the wind dies? You are becalmed. The peapod, accustomed to a taut painter, drifts alongside. We aren't getting anywhere! We may even be going backward!

Well, . . . Is that so bad? We aren't going backward very fast. Unless we are in imminent peril, being becalmed can be quite peaceful. On the Maine coast we are almost certain to be in a pleasant place: Penobscot Bay, for instance, the Camden Hills standing up to the west and the hump of Isle au Haut showing over Vinalhaven. Or off Matinicus, seeing the coast as Captain John Smith saw it in 1614. Or in Englishman Bay, where to the south and east we see the bare dome-shaped islands of Foster Channel and the white lighthouse on the long snake of the Libby Islands.

The wind will come in again. A hard blue line will show on

the horizon. The silky sea will show distant cat's paws. The pennant hanging slack at the masthead will lift a bit and drop. The main boom will creak across and slat on the other side. A little ripple creeps toward us. We feel a cool breath, the hard line comes closer, and in another five minutes we are on our way, the sails are full, and the helmsman calls,

"Sam, will you pass up my jacket on the starboard bunk?" This is too good to spoil with an engine.

What about coming into harbors, picking up moorings, coming alongside wharves? For years, before engines were invented, good seamen sailed into harbors and alongside wharves. When the clipper ship *Red Jacket* came into Liverpool after setting a record for an Atlantic crossing, she took a line from a tug at the mouth of the Mersey, but she sailed so fast that the tug couldn't keep the line taut. When she reached her wharf, Captain Asa Eldridge backed his topsails, passed lines ashore, and warped her alongside. Captain Sharp sailed the big Gloucester schooner *Adventure* into tiny Matinicus Harbor and anchored her in precisely the right place. I saw Captain Boyd Guild sail the big sloop *Georgie C. Bowden* into New Harbor and lay her alongside the wharf; and a party boat skipper in Southwest Harbor, sailing alone, coolly backed his sloop alongside a float by backing his staysail first on one side and then on the other.

All this time the engine has been sulking in the bilge, apparently ignored, unappreciated, and uncared for. But such is not the case. That engine cost a lot of money, is carefully nourished, and, when called upon, is very much appreciated.

In our part of Maine, they frequently turn off the wind at five o'clock. A party becalmed, or nearly so, within sight of our landing asks us where is the best place to eat, talks of steak versus lobster, of daiquiri versus Scotch. Everyone objects to starting the motor. And everyone appreciates my decision to do so.

There are places, too, where it is no fun to be becalmed.

Between the Cape Cod Canal and Scituate, for instance, there is nothing to look at ashore but the low hills behind Duxbury and the dunes on Plymouth Beach. One soon tires of trying to see the Pilgrim Monument at Provincetown, and Massachusetts Bay can be very hot. Express cruisers, motorsailers, and fishing launches agitate the water and the air. Let's fire her up!

There are times in the fog when the engine is called into action. If the wind is very light so the vessel makes only about 2 knots, the effect of the tide becomes significant, and the knot-meter becomes increasingly unreliable. Unless one is sure of his position, in home waters and only a short distance from his next mark, he would do well to proceed at a known speed on a known course—under power.

On the other end of the scale, there are times when stick and string, rag and rope, just won't do the job. Try to beat out of the narrow channel at Nantucket or the mouth of the Annisquam River or the Kennebec against the tide and a steep chop. In a low-powered auxiliary, even with a stout engine, it is a slow, wet, and bouncy business.

Occasionally a situation arises, either through bad luck or bad judgment, where the engine alone will save the ship. Mary and I came out of Winter Harbor near Schoodic under power on a windless afternoon. As we rounded Grindstone Neck, we got a bit of a breeze, shut off, and sailed up Frenchman Bay in an increasing southerly. Off Ironbound Island, it came in very brisk indeed. We headed in for Bar Harbor to windward of the Porcupines, and it came on to blow hard—too hard. We found ourselves quite close to a lee shore, carrying too much sail, and making more leeway than we liked. The lee deck was solidly under water, the chop, now running 3 feet high, pounded our bow to leeward. I had to spill wind from the mainsail to keep the coaming out of the water, thus radically reducing the driving power of the sail. Mary crawled forward and got the jib down, blessing the downhaul. This increased *Eastward*'s tendency to head into the wind and further reduced the efficiency of the sails. Lining up the end of Long Porcupine Island with the shore beyond showed we were not going to make it. With *Eastward* heeled to the coaming, the wind blowing off the top of the sail, and the mainsail all aluff, we did not have speed and power enough to tack against the cresting chop. Nor was there room enough between us and the lee shore to swing the other way and jibe. I couldn't leave the wheel. Obviously it was time to try the engine. Mary climbed down the hatch, opened and closed the essential petcocks, and hit the starter, and that stout old Atomic 4 sprang to life. This gave us power enough to squeak by the end of the island and into Bar Harbor. Watchers had thought we would be wrecked for sure and had called the Coast Guard, but they aborted the mission before the picket boat arrived.

There certainly will be times when we want the Iron Topsail and we will want it to respond at once to the click of the switch. What kind of engine should it be? I am a little ashamed that I did not give the matter the consideration it deserved. I decided on diesel in spite of our successful experience with the Atomic 4. That engine ran very well, but only because we gave it constant attention and practically rebuilt it over the years. Also, it is a delightfully simple machine and can usually be restored to health with a screwdriver and a 6-inch adjustable wrench. This is not true, however, of most modern gasoline engines, which, like the diesel, need the attention of a skillful mechanic.

The higher temperatures and pressures at which the diesel runs and the tighter tolerances to which it is machined usually mean it must be lifted out of the boat for any but the simplest repairs. However, a diesel engine would be less likely to explode than a gasoline engine, and people with diesel engines extol their reliability. So despite the higher cost, and on these rather vague and insubstantial reports, we decided on diesel.

But what diesel? I had not the least idea. Ralph recommended the Yanmar, a name I had not even heard before. I asked around, visited Chase Leavitt in Portland, collected brochures. The Yanmar brochure said it was the best engine ever conceived by the mind of God or constructed by the hand of man. The other brochures said the same of their engines. A man I met in the locker room at the YMCA said his brother had a Yanmar and liked it real well. I consulted Ralph further. He had had good experience with the Yanmar and could get one at a good price. Well . . . if Ralph liked it, I guessed that was good enough for me. What a numb-head way to make an important decision!

Or perhaps it was a very sound way after all.

So much for engines.

# VI

## GETTING READY

B Y NOVEMBER I FELT IT WAS ABOUT TIME TO GET THIS schooner started. On a soft, Indian summer afternoon, I went down on the shore in front of our house where a big old tree, roots and all, had drifted in last spring and lay on the rocks near high-water mark. We had tied it to a tree to prevent its becoming a hazard to navigation. It was about 15 inches in diameter at the butt, about 30 feet long, and a spiky tangle of broken limbs and torn roots. Where the roots swept off from the trunk should provide several knees suitable for gaff jaws.

Up to the garage for chain saw.

Cut off the tree about 4 feet above the root. That's progress!

Up to the garage for steel wedge and maul. Start the wedge amidst the tangle of roots where the grain looks right. Draw off and swing the maul at it. The wedge starts down, and a split shows along the grain. Haul off, swing the maul overhead, and hit that wedge again a solid whack. That's building a schooner!

Another six whacks and the wedge goes no farther. Nor will it come out.

Up to the garage for two more wedges. By following the grain where it started to split, beat in the second wedge and release the first. That's progress. Now put in the first below the second and that should get her.

Second wedge stuck. What is happening on the other side of the root?

Up to the garage again for a pry and a wrecking bar. Roll the stubborn root over. Small end of one wedge visible. Beat in third wedge next to it. Second wedge falls out, but the grain runs crooked and into another spike of the root. Fire up the chain saw and saw that off. Only one wedge stuck now. The grain appears more knotted, gnarled, and twisted than at first—really not suitable for gaff jaws.

The tide is rising and the sun is sinking. I need to get that wedge out.

Hit the root an almighty whack with the sharp edge of the maul. Now the maul is stuck. Twist it out? The handle of the maul breaks off just behind the head. Hit the head of the maul sideways with the axe. Bad for the axe, but the maul head comes out. Hit the wedge sideways with the head of the maul. No action. Didn't really think there would be.

The tide is creeping in between the rocks at my feet, and the sun is in the trees across the bay. Desperately hit the wedge a roundhouse swing with the wrecking bar. Hit it again on the other side. The wedge comes away.

Hastily get the tools on high ground. Carry them up the bank in the dusk.

"Where have you been all afternoon?" Mary asks.

"Building a schooner."

TWO DAYS LATER, C&B Marina, which kept *Eastward* in the winter, hauled her out and put her in a shed. I sopped out the last of the bilge water with a sponge, a wet and dirty job, and the last thing I could do for her.

Looking ahead to the spring, I could see *Dorothy Elizabeth* rolling into town on a trailer with no place to go. The ideal solution would be to have her at the yard of Paul E. Luke, Inc., next to our house. I called Frank Luke, current owner of the yard.

His father, Paul, had established the yard before World War

II and before and after the war had built gold-plater yachts for William Warner, John Alden, Sparkman & Stevens, Murray Peterson, Aage Nielsen, and other prominent designers. He had established a reputation for outstanding craftsmanship in wood. When most yards turned to production fiberglass, Paul turned to building custom aluminum yachts for the same designers, saying, "I would rather build one Cadillac than a thousand Fords."

Paul's family was very much a part of the business. His wife, Verna, managed the office, met sudden emergencies, and entertained customers. Their children, John, Frank, and Peggy, set bungs after school and later moved on to more sophisticated jobs. John ran the machine shop and later established his own business nearby, building aluminum lobster boats, "lobster yachts," and launches. He could, did, and can fabricate anything out of any metal.

Frank took over the yard when Paul retired, but by that time the market for aluminum yachts in the United States had collapsed under pressure from Spain, Korea, and Holland. He turned to building feathering propellers, elegant cabin heaters, stoves, and Luke anchors. Luke's feathering propellers have blades geared into a hub so that when the boat is going faster than the engine would drive it, the blades turn edgeways to the water. When the motor is driving the boat, the blades automatically turn the other way so that they drive the boat. I was interrupted in Frank's office one day by a call from a customer in Holland.

The cabin heaters are neat little stoves built of copper, some with pretty Dutch tiles, and lined inside with soapstone. They burn oil or briquets. His cook stoves, some with ovens, may be hung in gimbals to stay level when the boat heels, and burn whatever the owner specifies. All are custom made. During the summer there is often a customer's yacht alongside his float.

The Luke anchor is a conventional Herreshoff anchor, but it

is built in three pieces: flukes, shank, and stock. These are each light enough to handle easily but when brought on deck and assembled make a heavy storm anchor. Others make similar anchors, but as far as I know, Frank Luke is the man to see. He also does a considerable business in yacht storage, maintenance, and repair.

On top of that, Frank is a good seaman, having sailed a number of offshore delivery trips and ocean races, and he is one of the most generous, cheerful, and witty people in town. Once, the two of us were paddling ashore from *Eastward* with a visiting yachtsman in an aluminum dinghy with an aluminum oar in a thunderstorm—a hazardous business at best. As wet as rain could make us and somewhat relieved not to have been fried alive by lightning, Frank and I walked up the wharf. Our visitor ran ahead of us in a hurry to get under cover. "City kid," said Frank.

Another time, my mooring was caught down, and I asked Frank who could dive on it for me. He volunteered to do it and cleared the underwater tangle in short order. When I asked him the cost, he said, "Let it accumulate." He put a new cable in my come-along. "Let it accumulate." I made it up to him as best I could, but numerous contributions to our safety, health, and welfare are still accumulating.

So I dropped in on my neighbor Frank to ask for a parking place for *Dorothy Elizabeth*, still only a schooner on paper, when she should at last be expressed in wood. Also, I needed a place to lay out the spars so I could do the rigging. Finally, I needed a place to store her under cover for the winter.

The answer was yes, yes, yes. He would be delighted to have her in his yard, and, furthermore, if I met problems in finishing her out, as time served, he and his crew would help me. He would step the masts, launch her, and provide space for the extensive launching party that would surely take place some time in the summer. This would all be, of course, on a commercial basis.

NEXT I VISITED HIS BROTHER John's boat shop, quite dark after the sunny day outside but illuminated by the blue flicker of a welding torch. John emerged from the protective mask and gave me a walk-around tour of an aluminum boat he had designed and was building for an oil company in South Africa, to be used as a tender for an oil rig and for tankers that lie offshore and load through a pipeline. She is about 36 feet long, a rugged-looking vessel built with a hard chine and so engineered that the aluminum plates need not bend significantly in more than one dimension. At the moment I came in, he had been welding a tank for someone who wanted it right away yesterday.

John is not one to be rushed or easily perturbed. After education at Maine Vocational and Technical Institute and working to exacting standards as manager of the machine shop in his father's yard, he had learned not to rush things unduly. The day when we moved into our new house next door to his, he advised us never to say we would do anything at a certain hour or even on a certain day. It would be good enough to say we would do it next week if we could get to it. So I asked him if he could do the spar ironwork for me when he could get to it conveniently. He thought likely that would be possible and asked for the detailed drawings, to give him an idea of what materials he would need.

After Thanksgiving, with seven people at the table consuming a huge bird, four pies, and ice cream with appropriate auxiliaries, and after cleaning up and speeding the parting guests, we visited Nat Wilson, sailmaker down the road a piece. As soon as you open his door, you smell rope, canvas, and tar, for he deals in traditional materials as well as Dacron and nylon. The loft is up a steep stair, at the top of which is a large bright room, perhaps 25 by 40 feet, with windows on three sides and a view over the yachts and slips of the marina, the commercial yard of Washburn & Doughty building big steel vessels, and the Damariscotta River. The floor is varnished like a bowling alley. Under one window is a sailmaker's bench and on the other sides are several heavy-duty sewing machines. On the floor I found a huge pile of very heavy canvas, a mizzen topsail for USS *Constitution*.

Nat happened to be in his little box of an office set off in one corner of the floor. He is a wiry, tense man of uncertain age. I have known him since he made *Eastward*'s second jib topsail more than 20 years ago, and he seems not to have changed a bit.

I showed Nat the sail plan for *Dorothy Elizabeth* and asked if he could find time to build a suit of sails for her between finishing fore and mizzen topsails for *Constitution* and June 1. That he agreed to do. We were really making progress on a schooner that thus far existed only as an idea expressed on paper.

The next consideration was steering gear. The simplest and cheapest solution was a tiller. Furthermore, with a tiller one has direct communication with the water going by the boat—or with the boat going through the water. In a way impossible with mechanical steering devices, with a tiller one can feel in his fingers the complex pressures acting on the rudder and sense how the vessel is responding.

On the other hand, in a strong breeze or with a sea on the quarter, a tiller can pull hard. When I was a small boy—and I *was* a small boy, so short my feet would not reach across the cockpit of my father's sloop *Dorothy*—we were running out of Islesboro before a brisk northwester. He was on the bow watching for bottom, and I was at the tiller. He motioned, then called to me, "Keep her off. Keep her off!" I had the tiller under my chin, and my feet were slipping across the cockpit floor. I couldn't keep her off, so we slid up on a sandbar. A charitable fisherman pulled us off, and in an attempt to make us feel better, told us J.P. Morgan had put *Corsair* on the same bar. Still, even a bigger person than I gets tired after steering with a tiller in a strong breeze. The principal objection to a tiller, though, is that it sweeps across the cockpit, seriously limiting seating space.

So if not a tiller, what? Three kinds of steering gear were considered: a quadrant with wires running through blocks under the quarters to a wheel, a worm-gear system, or a hydraulic system. The latter seemed too complicated and expensive for our small boat. The first, although only a little less sensitive than a tiller, is subject to failure. The wires taking sharp turns over the quarter blocks need frequent inspection for fatigue. The skipper, too indolent or preoccupied to inspect frequently, may find himself in an awkward position should a tiller line part. The remaining alternative, a worm gear, is really designed for a bigger vessel than ours, but the parts are rugged. We would not in 50 years strip the worm gear. Operation is simple. The whole rig can be inspected and lubricated by lifting the top of the wheel box. And there is enough friction in the worm gear and the carriage so that one can leave the wheel to trim a sheet while the vessel sails herself.

The story is told, I don't remember where, of a man sailing alone in a small yawl across Narragansett Bay, headed for the buoy off Point Judith. A gentle breeze rippled the sunny surface of the bay, and after an hour of pleasant sailing the skipper needed to use the head. He balanced the rig carefully by adjusting sheets, lashed the wheel, went below, and closed the head door, which was on the lee side. A drawer in the dresser opposite the head slid out and jammed the door. Pounding, shouting, kicking was useless. After he passed an hour in unhappy contemplation, the breeze increased a little, the yawl tacked herself, the drawer slid back, and the skipper went on deck to find the buoy close astern. There is something to be said for a vessel that will sail herself—if she is well trained.

So we decided on a worm gear, traditional on Gloucester schooners. A little research convinced us that the Lunenburg Foundry in Nova Scotia made the one we wanted and that the NAFTA treaty gave us a break on the duty. It took only a telephone call to order it.

Then blocks, parral beads, belaying pins. The marine hardware catalogues were of little help, for they showed only stainless steel blocks with plastic sheaves designed for racing boats and priced accordingly. They had no idea of what a parral bead was, and their belaying pins were little brass pins too small and too expensive for us. Another visit to Frank Luke revealed a locker with a dusty collection of stout ash blocks with bronze sheaves and roller bearings made years ago for the traditional wooden yachts that Paul was building then. They lacked straps and pins, which John would have made in the machine shop. Frank gave me a good deal on them—more accumulation—and John agreed to make the straps. A stainless steel bolt would do for a pin.

However, Frank did not have enough to outfit a schooner, so back to Lunenburg to the shop of A. Dauphinée. It was a delight and an inspiration to talk on the telephone with a very pleasant lady across the Bay of Fundy about lignum vitae blocks, parral beads, and 10-inch ash belaying pins. Price? We talked about that too, but that is all part of building a schooner.

# VII

## GETTING STARTED
## AT LAST

O N JANUARY 8, 1997, RALPH CALLED TO SAY THAT THE lead keel had arrived; oak for the wood keel and frames and cedar for the planking had arrived. He had painted the shop floor and would be starting to lay down the lines for *Dorothy Elizabeth* on the coming Friday. We were actually starting to build a schooner. We had to be there. But the weather report for Friday was dismal—snow, sleet, and freezing rain. We reluctantly decided to put off the trip.

At four o'clock Friday morning, however, we woke to hear rain. Certainly we could not stay home in the mere rain with our schooner actually taking shape. Once we were on the road, the conditions deteriorated. Rain at our house next to salt water turned to slushy snow in Boothbay and to hard-packed snow on Route 27. But having started, we were not about to go back. Route 1 would be better. It was, but not much. All the way to Bucksport, where we made a pit stop, it was 4-wheel drive. (It seems a lot of our life has been lived in 4-wheel drive.) At Ellsworth the snow turned to rain, and we rolled up to Ralph's on a bare road about lunchtime. We ate our sandwiches with him in his living room; his house is next to the yard.

Bill Tefft, the photographer who was to record our vessel's construction for *WoodenBoat*, was not due until 3:30, so nothing could be done until then.

We asked Ralph how he had got into boatbuilding in the first place. Boatyards were always a part of Southwest Harbor life and a part of his life. He had asked boatbuilders how they did things but found that they were good at doing them but not at explaining. He learned by watching. Later, when he got stuck, he just sat down and puzzled it out.

As a boy and a young man he worked summers for summer people in Northeast Harbor, first sailing their small boat and later the schooner *Niliraga*. Thus he saved enough money so that when he wanted a lobster boat, he could build his own. He launched her on May 1, 1952. Two months later, someone asked him to build a boat and he couldn't wait to get started. Then he had a serious illness that laid him up for two years, but he started building boats again as soon as he could.

In 1962 he built the 33-foot Friendship sloop *Hieronymus*, the first of his yachts.

In the late 60s, fiberglass boats were being built quickly and less expensively than wooden boats. Ralph decided not to waste his experience and talent. He continued building wooden boats, for which there was a small but persistent demand.

Then, his neighbor Jarvis Newman asked him to help rebuild the shaky old Friendship sloop *Venture*. Since then he has rebuilt at least four other sloops, one of which was *Dictator*, built in 1904. Jarvis had bought her in Stonington, filled her with styrofoam so she could not sink, and had towed her awash to Southwest Harbor. He and Ralph rebuilt her entirely and Jarvis used her as a plug to build fiberglass *Dictators*. Ralph also has built at least five other Friendship sloops since *Hieronymus* as well as at least one schooner and numerous lobster boats. He has become so well known an authority on wooden boat construction that he was officially consulted on the recent reconstruction of USS *Constitution*.

At this point we adjourned to the shop to wait for Bill Tefft. Ralph went right to work cutting a notch in the stem of the English-type cutter to take the bronze fitting for the bobstay. He used a very sharp chisel, took out only a shaving at a time, and frequently tried the edge of the chisel on his thumb. He paused often to try the fitting in the notch. Richard was paying the seams of a small sloop, nearly finished. He wore yellow rubber gloves to keep his fingers from getting stuck up with seam compound, "and also this stuff isn't very good for you." The seams were narrow and even. Behind him they were nearly invisible.

A boy about high school age, with his baseball cap on backward—cool—was cutting bungs on a drill press. Like the others, he moved deliberately but made the chips fly. Andrea was making floorboards for the cockpit of the little sloop. At a long bench a young man was planing a mast, now eight-sided. With a long smoothing plane, he walked the length of the spar, the pine-scented shavings curling up and falling away.

We kept looking at the white-painted panel on the floor, wondering how the lofting for a 28-foot schooner could be done on a panel only about 15 feet square.

Lofting is the process of enlarging a vessel's lines, drawn on a piece of paper, to life size so patterns can be made from which the timbers of the vessel are cut. Traditionally, it is a tedious and painstaking operation performed on hands and knees, with a rule measuring to sixteenths of an inch and battens that are bent around the established points to fair out the lines. Not all builders are as careful as Ralph and Richard.

On the white plywood Ralph and Richard Stanley laid sheets of plastic with the lines of our boat already expanded to life size by computer. To begin with, they used only the sheets for the bow. Two of the sheets did not appear to line up by $\frac{1}{32}$ inch.

"What are you going to do about that?" I asked.

"Fudge it," said Richard. "That's what boatbuilders are for."

They laid a piece of building paper over the outline of the stem and marked on it the waterline and several other reference points to be sure it could be laid down again in exactly the same place. The paper was moved out of the way. Now a batten was bent along the line of the stem and held with spring wooden sticks thus:

Lofting the stem: Building paper will be slid under the batten and the line of the batten marked on it.

Lofting jig

WHEN THE BATTEN lay precisely along the line, the paper was slid under the batten and lined up with the reference marks. A pencil line was drawn on the paper along the line of the batten. The paper was removed and the same process repeated for the inner line of the stem and for the lines where the planking would come to the stem both inside and out—that is, the beard line and the rabbet line. With the last line drawn, the paper was cut out in the shape of the stem, ready to be laid on the oak and the oak sawn out.

It was snowing again and getting dark, but we stayed to see the completed pattern for the actual shape of *Dorothy Elizabeth*'s stem, the part that would meet the seas first.

ON OUR NEXT VISIT, February 3, we saw actual progress in wood. Ralph pointed to a 4-foot pile of chips and sawdust.

"There's your boat," he said. I must have shown my surprise and perhaps disappointment. He added that he kept the pieces of green oak buried in sawdust to keep them from drying out too fast and checking. He was cutting a concave curve in an 8-by-8 piece of the deadwood to make an aperture in which the propeller would turn. He worked first with a wide chisel, taking out chips about an eighth of an inch thick. I picked one up. It was wet, smelled, and tasted a bit sour. It was gray oak, botanically red oak, but Maine-grown red oak is often much less acid and less subject to rot than oak grown farther south.

Ralph's chisel approached the line of the curve that had been drawn from the pattern. Mary asked how he would cut that concave curve. Richard picked up a small plane with a convex blade and took a swipe with it.

"We got to show these fellas how to do it."

Ralph used that plane, a smaller chisel, and a power plane, working that heavy piece of oak down to the line as carefully, as precisely, as if it were to be a piece of fine furniture and not something to spend its life under water and out of sight. The plane was so sharp, he could cut across the grain without chipping a sliver off the far side. He kept trying the cut with a square to be sure it was square to both sides. It was.

I admit to having been a little disappointed in an apparently unproductive day. There was little to see in the construction of a schooner but a pile of chips and a great rough piece of oak whose

Keel assembly: The lead keel lies on top of the wood keel.
Pieces of the deadwood lie ready.

curves and intersecting planes were hard to fit to our concept of a vessel. The next visit, however, showed more obvious progress.

Across several horses lay *Dorothy Elizabeth*'s wooden keel, nearly 18 feet long, and on top of it a great slug of dark gray lead 9 feet long, with its ends cast to fit the coming deadwood. Ralph and Jonathan, another of the workers in the yard, were buttering the keel with white lead, then doing the same to a heavy piece of deadwood. They set the deadwood on the keel and slid it into the place made for it in the lead, for at this stage the boat was being built upside down. Richard appeared with a bronze bolt about 18 inches long and ¾ inch in diameter. He set the end in a hole in the deadwood and tunked it gently with a maul. It slid easily through the deadwood and hit precisely the hole drilled for it in the keel. Just before it came home, he wrapped around it under the head a length of cotton soaked in white lead. When it was seated solidly, he set up a nut on the other end and squeezed a bead of white lead from the seam. Neatly and expeditiously done with no haste and little conversation.

We stayed all afternoon to watch most of the rest of the deadwood slide together. Where several pieces had to go on top of each other—under each other, because the "boat" was upside down—the bolt was not long enough to go all the way through. Instead, it came down into a hole bored athwartships. A nut was fitted in the hole and tightened. Later, the hole would be plugged from each side.

Lest one conclude that perfection is possible on this planet, one bolt was too short. The nut could not catch the thread. The bolt was backed off a few inches and Richard crawled underneath to counterbore the hole with a heavy electric drill. The bit jammed, swung the handle around, and rapped Richard on the jaw. It was quite a sharp rap, but Richard went right back at it, finished the job, and set up the nut.

We departed in the winter dusk, leaving the keel and dead-

wood of our schooner bolted in place. The piece we had seen Ralph hollowing out with his plane was now looking entirely natural, its previously incomprehensible planes and angles part of our schooner, upside down to be sure.

But right side up, a revelation! A week later we opened the shop door and entered a cathedral. Before us lay the timbers we had seen assembled a week earlier, but now right side up with the lead properly on the bottom where the lead should be. And the stem swung up and up in a powerful curve, from the keel to the head of the goddess we could all but see under the vaulted roof of the shop. We knew, we deeply knew, we had a schooner.

# VIII

## S P L I C I N G   W I R E

ONE WINTER OUR THERMOMETER CURLED UP IN THE bottom of its bulb for most of February, and the whole of Linekin Bay froze over. At the end of the Washington's Birthday weekend, the little red line climbed all the way to 20°F. We stopped at a gasoline station in Wiscasset. The proprietor came out to pump gas in his shirtsleeves, announcing enthusiastically, "The winter's broke."

February has gone. It snows still, but snow doesn't last long under March sun. We begin to smell mud, and winter projects are winding down.

We had undertaken to become "computer literate," at least enough to decide intelligently whether we wanted to buy a computer. We took a computer course in the adult education program taught by my brother Donald. Mary ran into a problem that she mentioned to a third-grade girl whom she was tutoring in reading.

"Oh," said the child, "we had that in first grade." We finished the last class by unscrambling the Gettysburg Address, which it had taken a genius to write and another genius to scramble. We decided we were not ready for the computer.

We finished teaching our own adult education course, "Poetry for Dessert." The last class was illuminated by my brother's recitation of Ruth Moore's "The Night Charlie Tended Weir." He and I work together.

76

I attacked the woodpile with chain saw, axe, maul, and wedge but put the last of it off until later, for *Dorothy Elizabeth* pressed. The wire for the standing rigging had arrived.

I bolted my little splicing vise to the shop bench and screwed the legs of the bench to the floor. That bench was about to take some strain. I borrowed from Nat Wilson a bigger splicing vise, nailed that to the floor, and then rigged a tackle—two single blocks—to a stout post that held up the whole house. I canvassed the hardware stores for the most powerful wire cutters in town. There is a lot of getting ready to splicing wire rigging.

At last, as crocuses pushed up little green spears, I bent a piece of 7 x 7⁵⁄₁₆ wire rigging around a thimble and clamped it in the big vise. This wire is tough stuff. It consists of six strands laid around a stiff wire core. Each strand is made up of seven little wires. It can be bent, but it surely doesn't like to be bent and will snap back and bite you if it can. The vise has three jaws, two to squeeze the wire to the sides of the thimble and one to hold it against the top of the thimble. They must be tightened more or less equally in order to force the wire snugly against the thimble. Then the standing part of the wire must be hauled taut by the tackle to keep the strands tightly together and to prevent the splice from becoming all "baskety."

Now, with everything set up and ready, with wire cutters and marlinespike in hand, I take the first actual physical step in my part of building *Dorothy Elizabeth*. This piece of wire will go to sea with her.

There is a mystique to splicing wire, held by people who have never done it and suggestive of a sweaty brow and bloody hands. Not so. I first saw it done in 1937 one hot, calm morning in Portland Harbor. I found that we needed a new gaff bridle, a short piece of wire with an eye on each end. I was referred to Tim Coulen, rigger. He went at it enthusiastically, with flying fingers, spike, and pliers. Nothing to it! I hadn't the least idea of how he had done it. Afterward, he suggested a beer. We adjourned from the loft to the bar below and drank Manz beer, which he taught me to dose with salt.

I learned the skill myself while working as a rigger's helper at Bath Iron Works during the war. On pleasant days our crew was set to rigging life nets under the rails of destroyers, but on rainy days we worked in the loft on wires to go alongside the ladders in the officers' quarters. These wires were eye-spliced on each end, then parceled, served, and covered with canvas. That is, the bare wire was wrapped with a canvas strip, then wound tightly with marline and, over that, covered with canvas. My job was to take a long canvas strip, tuck the edges inward and crease them, then wrap the strip around the wire and sew the edges together with a herringbone or a "baseball" stitch. A bit tedious, but the loft was a quiet and pleasant place to work, smelling of tar, rope, and canvas. The crew varied from young men and women learning the trade to older men who had been to sea on big schooners and square-riggers. There was a good deal of airy persiflage flying about.

To a professional wrestler in the crew:

"What would you do if you got in the ring with Man Mountain Dean?"

"I'd make a lunch while he was getting a meal."

"How's your wife and my children?"
"Wife's all right but the children's kind of foolish."

"It's five minutes to the whistle. Why are you quitting?"
"I got dirty on company time. I wash up on company time."

AND ALL THE WHILE I am sitting on a bench with a coil of wire and a strip of canvas on my knees, making even stitches and pulling them snug.

When I was out of wire or canvas, one of the older gentlemen taught me to splice wire. I learned that a marlinespike is not like an ice pick but tapers gently to a rounded, flattened point with sharp edges. My mentor slipped the spike under a strand easily, then rotated the spike around the wire a full turn so it ran up the wire away from the thimble. He gave a quick twist to the strand to be tucked, passed it around the wire in the same way the spike had traveled to take the twist out of it, slid it in beside the spike, pulled it tight, and turned the spike back down the wire, driving the strand ahead of it hard up against the thimble. Then he "cut it in" with the sharp edge of the spike to drive it down hard and flatten it out.

When I tried it, I couldn't get the spike under a strand in the standing part of the wire. I pushed, pried, and strained.

"Don't fight the wire," he said. "Go with it." He showed me just how to hold the spike, how to slide the edge between the strands, push hard, and lift the strand. Then I had to master that twist to get the turn out of the strand so it would lie flat and to slip the end under the strand parallel to the spike rather than to pry up the strand brutally and try to jam it through. After patient coaching, a good deal of practice, and several ruined pieces of wire paid for by the United States Navy, I somehow acquired the feel, the rhythm.

More than half a century later, I find the wire stubborn, resistant, unwilling, and slippery. The spike slides sideways and skins a knuckle. At last I force the spike under the first three strands and twist the spike down the wire. I pass the first strand to be tucked around the wire to take the twist out of it and slip it in behind the spike, then twist the spike back to drive the strand tight against the thimble, just like the old days. I didn't get the twist out of the strand very well, and it didn't go as tightly against the thimble as it should have, but it was in there and it was not going to come out. The next strand went under two, and each of

ABOVE: The first strand tucked. OPPOSITE, TOP: Cutting it in.
OPPOSITE, BOTTOM: The first complete tuck. Notice that the strands
are tucked *with* the lay of the wire, not against it as they are in rope.

the four others under one, and that was the first tuck. It didn't lie
as flat as it should, but it was there to stay.

On successive tucks I found myself fighting again to get the
spike into the wire. I had to push, pry, and struggle. Under such
pressure, one tends to personify the opposition, to call it bad
names, finally to triumph over it. After several splices, however,
my hands remembered what they had learned in the rigging loft
in Bath and what they had practiced later on *Eastward*'s rigging.
I applied the force more smoothly and in the right places and

Roger F. Duncan

with the right twist. Less emotion and smoother splices.

Nevertheless, pay attention! If you get a strand under the wrong strand in the standing part, the Gordian Knot will look like the bow in your shoestring. Get the spike under the wayward strand and try to pry it out from where it doesn't belong. Get a grip with the pliers. They slip over the slippery wire. Try again, try again. At last the strand is pried or dragged out, but the twist is out of it and the individual wires are kinked and tortured out of their accustomed shape. Now tuck it into the mangled standing part where it belongs. It won't come tight; the kinks prevent its sliding into place. Pry, pull with the pliers. Yank with the pliers. Jab with the spike, and at last, before it gets worse, leave it as the best that can be done, with its twists and kinks lurking to bedevil you the next time you come to tuck it.

I tucked each of the six strands four times, then cut out three wires from each strand and tucked each again for a "locking tuck," to taper the splice, which prevents its catching on things, and for style. This is going to be a stylish little vessel.

That splice wasn't perfect. Nothing is. When the strain comes on it, it may stretch a little; but the greater the strain, the more tightly the strands of the standing part will squeeze down on the strands tucked under them. With all its imperfections on its head, that splice will hold.

To finish the job, the splice must be parceled and served. Here is an easy and pleasant conclusion. First I take my heaviest hammer and beat the splice hard and often to beat down the cut-off ends of the wires and all the humps, bumps, and hubbles that should not be there but always are. Then I wrap the splice with a strip of canvas, starting at the thimble and winding with the lay of the wire. On top of that, I wrap a layer of tarred friction tape. Before the days of stainless steel wire, this was done to keep water out, which prevents the splice from rusting. With stainless wire, I do it because . . . because it is the proper way to

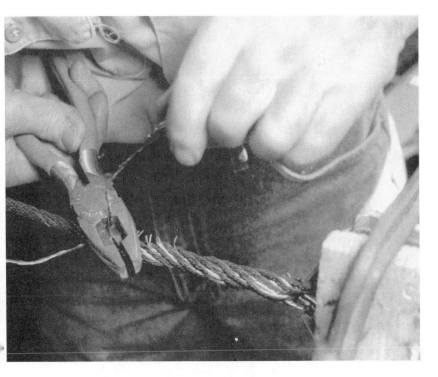

**The finished splice**

do it, and it makes the finished job look better. Then the splice is served with marline; that is, marline is wound very tightly over the parceling against the lay of the wire and toward the thimble.

Marline is properly Italian hemp twine, two stranded and laid left handed and soaked in tar. When wound very tightly with a serving mallet, the tar squeezes out of the marline and makes an even coat over the whole splice. However, proper marline is almost unavailable. What you get is nylon twine impregnated with something that smells rather like kerosene and doesn't squeeze out. It must be tarred afterward.

**Hit it hard**

There is a proper way to wrap that marline around the wire. Years ago, before the war, I anchored in Home Harbor, a small, snug spot inhabited in summer by two families of lobstermen with whom we had become acquainted over several visits. The serving on one of my shrouds had worn out. I undertook to replace it by winding marline around the splice by hand, passing the ball of marline around the shroud for each turn, pulling it as tight as I could, holding it somehow with a thumb, and passing the ball around again. One of the fishermen came alongside in his punt, watched awhile, and said as he departed,

"Doin' and undoin' makes work for damned fools."

Serving

He was right, of course. That serving fell off of its own weight. Later, in the rigging loft at Bath, I found out how it was done properly.

The marline is wound around the serving mallet in such a way as to provide enough friction to pull the marline very tight. A proper rigger will have a boy to pass the ball of marline around the wire for every turn he takes, but most of us rig a reel attached to the handle of the mallet.

Now, in my own shop, with the end of the marline tucked under the final four turns, yanked tight, and cut off, I had finished the first splice in *Dorothy Elizabeth*'s standing rigging. This was her inner bobstay and would go to sea with her. An extra libation for that!

Perhaps now it is too late to ask why I would splice wire rigging when swaged fittings are easier and quicker. The answer is unconvincing. In a swaged fitting, the end of the wire is slipped into a tube with an eye on the end and then run through a press that squeezes the tube very tightly against the wire, so tightly that it will never pull out. I never heard of one that did. However, the fitting and the wire are often of different metals. Especially on the lower ends of the rigging, salt water collects on the top of the fitting and evaporates, leaving a deposit of salt. In the presence of an electrolyte like a strong solution of salt, different metals set up a galvanic action that corrodes one of the metals. Once in a while you hear of a fitting that cracks or lets go or requires renewal. Splices, on the other hand, have only one metal. If properly done, they are neat and seamanlike. Most important, I like them better and I can do them myself.

# IX

## B E N D I N G   F R A M E S

A S THE CROCUSES BROKE INTO BEAUTIFUL BLOOM, CAME
another sign of spring, the Maine Boatbuilders Show, in
Portland. After standing in line in the cold rain for a suitable
time, I entered a huge barnlike structure among aisles of power-
boats, glistening fiberglass sides towering to flybridges. Each had
a flight of steps, some hung with signs urging visitors to remove
their shoes, more perhaps as an act of worship than to preserve
the teak decks. In this plastic desert were some welcome oases,
however. Here was a wooden peapod beautifully put together
and finished. There was Frank Luke's booth with an exhibit of
galvanized Luke anchors, perhaps the only galvanized iron in the
show. The Pert Lowell booth advertised mast hoops. I had tried
for them at Lunenburg when I bought the blocks, parrals, and
belaying pins but was told that the Indians that used to make
them had given them up in favor of making curios to trap
tourists. I ordered fifteen 7-inch mast hoops for our new
schooner. Numerous other booths advertised wizard electronics
that bounced waves off satellites hundreds of miles aloft and
would display on a screen a chart showing one's track, position,
course, and speed. All it did not show was how long you might
be laid up at a boatyard getting the wizard repaired.

Below a low lintel leading to an ill-lighted attic was
Traditional Marine Outfitters, a Canadian firm manufacturing
bronze fittings like port lights, bullet blocks, and bow chocks.

There I found a ball of real marline at a prohibitive price and a 10-inch marlinespike, which I bought without asking the price. I had had one that I bought when I was working at Bath Iron Works during the war, but I dropped it overboard and it couldn't swim. If I was not making real progress on *Dorothy Elizabeth*, at least I was maintaining momentum.

The momentum increased. On succeeding days we gathered speed. On March 27 when we walked into Ralph's shop we saw the backbone assembled as before and now painted with red lead. There was a rabbet, a groove, cut in the length of it on each side to take the garboard, the first plank. The angle changed smoothly from bow to stern to fit the changing angle at which the plank would meet the stem, keel, and deadwood. Every 8 inches a slot was cut just above the rabbet to take the foot of a rib, known to boatbuilders as a frame or timber.

Above the red-leaded backbone rose a maze of boards and braces, none of which would ever go to sea. Straddling the keel was a series of wooden molds, each a cross section of the boat at a particular point, and over the top arched a strongback to hold the molds down tightly on the keel. From bow to stern, bent around the molds was a series of ribbands, wood strips each about an inch thick, to hold the molds from tipping forward or aft and, later, to give the frames their shape. By standing off a ways and squinting my eyes, I could get a pretty good idea of the shape the schooner would take, but it was all hazy, insubstantial, evanescent. The crew was busy doubling the ribbands to make each 2 inches thick. These ribbands were to take considerable strain as the frames were bent inside them.

We adjourned for lunch. Again we ate our sandwiches in Ralph's living room and talked of earlier days, of how until quite recently Little Cranberry Island had been a rather isolated community where people used words obsolete on the mainland, like "ken" for "know" and "rue," as a verb, meaning regret. Ralph

The battens are fastened to the stem and bent around
the molds to establish the schooner's shape.

called it "original Marblehead," whence had come early settlers
to Cranberry Island, but we agreed that even earlier Scotch-Irish
settlers in Marblehead had brought it to America with them. I
asked Ralph how he had become interested in history, for he has
written a number of articles on the history of Mount Desert, has
given a paper at a symposium of the Maine Maritime Museum,
and is an active member of the Mount Desert Historical Society.
He said he had always listened attentively to the stories his
grandmother had told him of the old days, and genealogy has
also been interesting to him. He has persistently followed up on

whatever leads and loose ends he could find. All very interesting, but Mary and I couldn't wait to get back to the shop.

We found there a feeling of anticipation. Something important was imminent. Collect a vast number of C-clamps, oil them, spin them open, and hang them on convenient ribbands. One seizes a well-oiled clamp by the handle, holds it vertically, handle up, and spins it. How? By a dexterous rotary motion that takes advantage of momentum to exploit the eccentric balance of the heavy clamp. Words are inadequate. You just grab it by the handle and spin it. Try it.

There are some things that cannot be described in words. You cannot *tell* a child how to ride a bicycle. You put her on it, hold it up, put her feet on the pedals. Still balancing the bike by the rear fender, you run down the sidewalk as she pedals. When you are about to drop dead, she rides away from you. Twenty, 40, 60 years later she can still ride a bicycle. It is the same with skating, swimming, sculling a punt, and spinning a clamp. Just do it and you will know how.

Andy fired up the stove with scrap wood to the not-so-subtle smell of wood smoke. Richard filled the boiler. This is a cubical steel box to the bottom of which is welded a U of pipe going down into the fire of the stove. From the top of the boiler goes a pipe to the steam box above, a horizontal wooden box about 8 feet long and 18 inches square with a shelf about halfway up.

Andrea is passing Ralph the frames, 2½-by-1-inch strips of oak 8 feet long, for him to pass through the screaming band saw. He is cutting each frame lengthwise to make two ½-inch pieces joined at the lower end by about 3 inches left uncut. Andy loads them into the steam box, now steaming vigorously.

The process slowed down while the frames cooked for about an hour. Staging was taken down and the planks stacked outside. Steps were placed on each side of the boat about amidships. The floor was swept. A box of nails was set on the keel on the inside.

Andy stoked the stove. Richard added water to the boiler. Steam rose from the steam box. The clock crept slowly, slowly, through its accustomed orbit.

Ralph and Richard climbed into the "boat." Andy opened the end of the steam box, with a gloved hand pulled out a frame, passed it, steaming, to Ralph. He jammed it into a notch cut in the keel. Andrea, outside, checked to be sure it was firmly seated in its notch and correctly aligned. Ralph seized the top of it and with his foot drove the frame hard out against the ribbands on the starboard side, pulling the top of it toward him. Andrea

**Richard bending in an after frame and someone ready to clamp it from outside.**

**The vessel timbered out. Battens, frames, molds and strongback in place.**

snapped a clamp on the frame and the lowest ribband and tightened it up while Jonathan clamped the next one above it. In the space of a little over a minute, the frame was clamped to the ribbands and nailed there, still wet and hot. Richard was doing the same thing on the port side. Before Richard had finished, Andy was passing Ralph another frame.

These frames were the vessel's skeleton. Like ribs, they defined, determined, and held the boat's shape now and henceforward through squall, storm, and shipwreck; through all the strains, twists, and wrenchings she must endure. As we stood to one side, we saw piece after piece of oak become a frame in our vessel. As Ralph and Richard moved forward inside the insubstantial confusion of molds, strongback, ribbands, and bracing, *Dorothy Elizabeth* was becoming the schooner that would go to sea. She had become so much of a vessel in one afternoon that we asked Ralph when he would be ready to launch her. He mentioned late April, noncommittally. To all of us, she had assumed a reality she had not had that morning.

### Here are Ralph Stanley's reflections on bending in frames:

IN THE PROCESS OF BUILDING A BOAT, the builder always sets goals to be reached as the building progresses. In steaming and bending the frame on a 35-foot lobster boat, the goal is to complete the job in a day. Needless to say, it is a long day, but the time involved to fire up the boiler another day puts the builder behind one more day in the schedule.

Timbering-out day starts early in the morning, usually before daylight, to fill the boiler and get the fire going. You can't fill the boiler the night before, as it is invariably freezing weather and the water would freeze in the boiler. After breakfast, the water is hot enough to produce steam. Ten or 12 timbers are already in the steam box, and after they have steamed an hour or so, they are ready to bend.

I usually bent the frames and fastened them to the ribbands from inside the boat, and usually had two helpers outside to tend the fire and boiler and to pass me hot timbers while replacing them in the steam box with cold ones. The helpers outside the boat clamped the timbers to the ribbands as I bent them in the proper position. When they were all clamped in place, I would nail them to the ribbands from inside. Needless to say, it is hot work and you work as fast as you can to get the timbers bent before they cool off. In a 35-foot lobster boat, there are 86 frames that have to be steamed and bent, taking 8 to 10 hours. It is a hot, tiring day.

We were always worried about having such a hot fire and were always very careful. We had a large piece of metal under the stove to catch any coals that might drop when putting more wood in the stove. Sometimes the sides of the stove would be red-hot.

We finished timbering one boat that I remember about 6:30 P.M. The stove was half full of red-hot coals, so we closed the stove to let it cool slowly. The boiler was still bubbling. Everything was cleared away from the stove and we left the shop. I went home, too tired to eat much. I took a bath and got myself cooled off. After resting awhile, I decided to go and check the shop as I usually did after timbering a boat. When I opened the shop door, I smelled smoke and, turning the light on, I could see layers of smoke in the air sort of like someone smoking a cigar, only it was not cigar smoke. I looked around but could not see any fire. To be safe, I dumped water on the floor around the stove. I figured the stove was shut too tight, so I adjusted the damper, turned out the lights, and went into my father's house and visited for half an hour. On leaving, I checked the shop again, and again I noticed layers of smoke. I left the doors open and aired the shop pretty well while I looked around again. I found nothing, so I closed the shop and went home. At home, I felt uneasy and I guess I waited an hour before going back to the shop. The layers of smoke were in the air again. I looked all over and still could find nothing burning. I aired the shop again and adjusted the damper again, and after one more look around I went to turn out the lights. As I reached for the switch, I hesitated and thought I might as well look again. As I walked by the stem of the boat, I heard a snap that sounded like wood burning, and the sound seemed to come from up over the stove. I had looked around the chimney as it went up through the roof but could see nothing. As I took another look, I got in a position where I could see behind the chimney better and I saw a beam of 2 x 12 hemlock fastened inside the studs about halfway up the chimney and about a half inch from it. It was all a-glow. I had a fire extinguisher and got a ladder, but the extinguisher would not put out the fire. I had a bucket of water and a tin can for a dipper, and I splashed water a dipper at a time and put the fire out. To make sure, I took my handsaw and cut that beam right out. That beam was about $\frac{1}{16}$-inch from burning through. If it had burned through, it would have created a draft and probably would have burst into flames, and the whole back end of the shop would have been on fire in about 10 minutes. Something surely kept me from pulling the light switch and leaving.

# X

## PLANKING

THINGS WERE MOVING FAST. WE HAD SEEN THE FRAMES bent in on Thursday, March 27. The weekend, Easter weekend, was devoted to hasty completion of tax forms, to busy kitchen work: lemon cake, bunny cake, ginger cookies for the church refreshment table, and to a fierce battle with a badly executed wire splice. But Monday morning, March 31, saw us back in Ralph's shop.

*Dorothy Elizabeth* stood before us, all her frames in place. Today planking was to start. When a boat is properly planked, it looks as if there were no trick to it—just like clapboarding a house. Each plank appears to be the same width as the ones above and below it. Just nail them on, one after another.

Now consider the matter more carefully. A boat, unlike a house, is fatter in the middle than she is in the bow. Notice that the planks are narrower in the bow, broader amidships, and taper again toward the stern. If you could see the boat out of the water, you would notice that the lower planks below the turn of the bilge in the stern are quite wide because the boat is deeper there. To make the planks look so neat and even, each plank must be tapered in just the right way.

There is another difference between a boat and a house. A boat is curved in every dimension, not only fore and aft but from keel to rail. Try to wrap an apple in a piece of paper without a wrinkle. It can't be done. Peel an orange by cutting meridians from stem end to navel end. You will see that each strip is narrow at the north pole, curves to the equator, and curves back to the south pole. Even then, the Grand Architect fashioned the strips so they will not lie quite flat. If it is so difficult to plank up an apple or an orange with paper, try it in wood on a vessel that must be watertight. The method of designing a plank so it will fit into its place is called *spiling*.

When we arrived on Monday morning, the two bottom planks (the garboards), one for each side, had been spiled, cut out on the band saw, and nailed together. Ralph was planing the edges to make them identical. Richard and a helper were cutting

**Andrea carefully fairing a frame to take the garboard plank.**

numerous sticks about 16 inches long whose purpose at this time was in no way apparent. Andrea with a very sharp little plane was fairing off the edges of the frames so the garboards would fit snugly against the full width of each frame. (This work on a big vessel is called *dubbing* and was usually done with an adze. A dubber must have a keen eye and a sharp adze. Such craftsmen were much in demand.)

Ralph took apart the two garboards and carefully plugged the nail holes with cedar pegs, which he whittled out with his knife. He then ran the garboards through the planer to reduce them to finished thickness and inspected the starboard one carefully. He drilled out a few big or loose knots and plugged the holes.

Andrea checked the frames by laying along a batten where the garboard would go and kept on trimming the frames with the plane—minutely. Richard was cutting wedges, again to no apparent purpose.

When the garboard is at last in place, its bottom edge must fit accurately into the rabbet in the keel at an angle that changes from aft forward. The rabbet has already been cut to this changing angle. Ralph now measured the angles of the rabbet at about 2-foot intervals and marked them on a stick. With his knife he cut notches in the lower edge of the garboard at the same 2-foot intervals at angles to correspond with those he had measured. Then he planed the edge of the garboard from notch to notch to notch, changing the angle by eye as he went, until the notches disappeared and the angle changed as smoothly as the rabbet. He left a small bevel in the edge of the garboard to take the caulking later.

All builders aren't as skillful or careful. It is reported that a caulker driving cotton into the garboard seam of a Friendship sloop in Wilbur Morse's shop found a place in the seam so wide that the cotton went right through. He picked up an old work glove from the chips on the floor in front of him and caulked that into the seam with the thumb sticking out. None of that in the Stanley shop.

Andrea now appeared satisfied that the garboard would lie fair against the full width of every frame. Richard and a helper set the garboard in place and held it by putting the aforementioned sticks inside, spanning the interval between two frames, and clamping the garboard in place. At first glance, the garboard, held only by a couple of clamps at the after end, didn't appear to fit at all. The forward end stuck way out from the frames and drooped; it had a weird curve that appeared to have no relation to *Dorothy Elizabeth*'s lines. No one seemed disturbed, and I had sense enough, rare in a superannuated schoolteacher, to keep my mouth shut.

However, as more sticks and clamps were put on farther forward, it looked better. The garboard is almost vertical at its after end where it lies against the vertical deadwood, but must twist to lying almost horizontal against the midship frames. Ralph had, of course, allowed for this in spiling.

These ruminations were interrupted.

Jonathan was fitting iron "dogs" to successive frames. These are something like heavy belt buckles arranged so they will slide down a frame but not up. Richard pushed an aforementioned wedge between the dog and the top of the garboard and tapped the wedge in to push the garboard down against the rabbet. He put a wooden pad on the top edge of the garboard to keep the top edge and the caulking seam fair; then, with a hacksaw blade, he felt along the seam where the garboard came down on the rabbet. If he struck a place too tight, the garboard came off, was planed down a shaving and mounted again. After more than a few hitches, Richard was heard to comment that the garboard might have been better spiled. Even boatbuilders, even very patient boatbuilders, have their frustrations.

At last Richard was satisfied that the garboard would come

OPPOSITE: Andrea driving home the fastenings.
ABOVE: The garboard plank in place.

down evenly on the keel. The wedges were driven hard under the dogs, the clamps tightened so the garboard lay fair against each frame and fitted precisely the changing angle of the rabbet. The weird angle of the forward end now lay naturally in its place, curving upward as the keel rose toward the stem.

With an electric drill fitted with a bit that bored a small hole for the shaft of the screw and had a larger end that counterbored for the head, Ralph drilled through the top of the garboard into each frame and through the bottom into the keel. A 1½-inch #12 bronze screw was set in each hole. Andrea drove them home with a chattering power screwdriver. The dogs and clamps were removed, and there she stood—the first plank on the starboard side. And it was lunchtime.

A snowstorm was predicted for the afternoon, so we fled home, singing old songs all the way.

THE NEXT WEEK went flying by. Caught on the wing: a very bad splice that I had to saw off and start again (it hangs on the shop wall, its six tortured tentacles writhing); a wild tale of seasick Indians from Hubbard's *Indian Wars*, which I wrote up for *The Working Waterfront*; a splice in the forestay before which I forgot to thread on the brass rings to take the staysail's jackline; a church service I wrote on Thoreau's *Civil Disobedience* for a speaker who forgot to set his watch ahead for Daylight Saving Time and turned up an hour late. . . .

But on Monday, April 7, back to the boat shop to find the crew working on the eighth plank up from the keel. I watched carefully while Ralph spiled the plank, and concluded that he established a line more or less along the middle of the place where the plank was to go and measured at close intervals down to the top of the plank below and up to where the plank above was to start, then transferred the measurements to the new plank and faired the curves with a batten. When he had cut out the plank on the band saw, it was hard to see how that curved and crooked board could assume the shape of another even plank in the succession of even planks now stepping up the side of *Dorothy Elizabeth*, but once clamped in place, driven down by wedges and fastened, it looked as if it had grown there. She was now about half planked from the keel to the rail.

Again a hectic week flew by. This week included a trip to Belmont Hill School, an independent secondary school in Massachusetts, where I used to teach and of which I am still an Incorporator. Our son, Bob, now owner of *Eastward*, came from Concord to grease seacocks and preside over her launching.

Splicing continued with increasing speed and accuracy. A box of wooden belaying pins, blocks, parral beads, deadeyes, and fairleads arrived April 9 from A. Dauphinée in Lunenburg, Nova Scotia. Every one is beautifully made and finished. I must press on—press on. There is not a moment to lose.

Meanwhile, the sweet cedar planking continued to climb up around the turn of *Dorothy Elizabeth*'s bilge and up her topsides. A week after our last visit, a shutter party seemed indicated.

When a wooden boat is planked, said the old man, she is half done. She looks more than half done. She looks complete. She stands on her keel in the shop, clear of the clutter of molds, ribbands, strongback, and staging, supported only by a few unobtrusive props under her bilge. The last plank to go on is called a *shutter* because many builders plank up from the garboard and down from the rail, leaving until last a plank just above the turn of the bilge. The closing in and fastening of that last plank is celebrated with a shutter party. Ralph planks from the keel to the rail, so the last plank is the top plank. Nevertheless, we felt we should have a shutter party.

That same old man said the shutter always goes in wet. A shutter party can be an extended and raucous celebration attended by the entire neighborhood. However, the character of the Stanley yard suggested a more modest recognition of the event. Mary baked cookies, fried doughnuts, and made a large Fochabers ginger cake for the event. I raided the supermarket for ginger ale, various colas, beer, several bottles of wine, and a jug of rum. Thus loaded, we added a bucket of ice at Ellsworth and arrived at the yard to find my brother Donald and his wife, Joyce, already present with camera and bagpipe. Our old friend Jill Evans, who had been a "camper" at a camp at which I had been sailing instructor in 1937, appeared by special invitation, as did Farnham and Gladys Butler, former boatbuilder and old friends from way back. Ralph's crew, his wife Marion and his daughter

Nadine, and friends and relatives of the crew added to the occasion. Bill Tefft, official *WoodenBoat* photographer, recorded the event on film.

Richard ignored the onlookers and the approaching festivities as he prepared the last two planks, one for each side, yet he seemed to be feeling the pressure and to be quietly enjoying the suspense.

The visitors turned their backs on the refreshments laid out on the bench and watched as Andrea sawed off the short end of the last plank and drove home the last screw. *Dorothy Elizabeth* was half done and looked magnificent and maidenly.

Everyone turned to the refreshments. My brother picked up

The shutter

the short end that Andrea had sawed off. He tuned up the pipes and marched up and down the ship in traditional manner as he played several selections, concluding with "Amazing Grace" and "Fair Harvard," in my opinion the best of pipe music. We left the shop bearing the conviction that we had built a boat.

The next morning we climbed the staging by the stern to watch Andrea and Jonathan sawing off the projecting tops of the frames and Richard fairing up the fashion pieces that completed the graceful curve where the side planking flows into the counter. The water would slip by her, scarcely disturbed by her easy passage.

**Richard and Ralph**

William Garvie

Enough of dreaming. Back then to life in East Boothbay: the early-morning swim to keep in shape, the chores of daily living, and now an editing job on the yearbook of the Friendship Sloop Society. I was still a member of the Society and editor of the yearbook. Half of the book was devoted to advertising and half to copy that I was to supply by May 1. Several pages had to be devoted to lists of sloops registered, officers, winners of last year's regattas, and to recipients of various awards. The rest of my half was to be filled by contributions sent in by members. Most of these contributions were surprisingly good, but all needed radical surgery, for which my experience as a secondary school English teacher qualified me admirably.

A neighbor offered a kerosene stove. We went to inspect it at his house on the shore, found it wouldn't do, but stayed to admire the North Atlantic Ocean stirred impressively by a spring northeaster of wind and rain.

Our health insurance agent called with a good proposition over which we spent several hours of arithmetic. Wire splicing continued, going better and better as hands and head fell into remembered rhythms. I had ahead of me two wire straps to make. I had an idea of how to do it, but I had never made one and dreaded having to get started. To avoid it, I pressed on vigorously with what I knew how to do.

Ralph called to ask how wide the side decks should be. Here was an important decision, and it was pressing. The side decks should be wide enough to walk on. Those on the Rozinante were far too narrow. *Eastward*'s are about right, but *Eastward* is a foot and a half wider than *Dorothy Elizabeth*. The wider the side decks,

---

Now, with the molds out and all the extraneous bracing removed, we could see the whole shape of the vessel. Looking down inside her, we admired the fine bow swelling easily into the buoyant waist, then turning up into the flat run.

the narrower the house, hence the less room below. But first things first. The boat is primarily for going to sea, only secondarily a place in which to live. So how wide should the decks be? What to do? Jump in the car and drive to the East Boothbay yard where *Eastward* lay alongside a float and measure her deck. At the narrowest place it is 15½ inches. But how will that be on a narrower boat? Really, we can't tell without seeing the boat, so with hands unwashed, in the middle of the morning, we drove to Ralph's shop.

We found continuing progress. Deck clamps and bilge clamps were in. These are timbers running the full length of the boat, fastened to the inside of the frames to give the structure longitudinal stiffness. When she is supported by a wave at each end, she tends to bend up at each end like a banana. When the wave is in the middle with her ends unsupported, she tends to droop, to *hog*. The deck clamp runs just below the top plank. The deck beams rest on it. The bilge clamps stiffen the vessel at the turn of the bilge.

Andrea and Ed were fitting floor timbers, a fussy job. The floor timbers sit on the keel and are fastened to planks from outside and drifted down into the keel. A *drift* is a rod driven into a hole too small for it. Once in, it is immovable. Each floor timber must fit the compound curve of the inside of the planking and the angle of the keel—all at once.

We climbed aboard *Dorothy Elizabeth* for the first time, and Richard gave us a guided tour. He showed us where the anchor bitt, masts, bridge deck, and wheel would come. The cockpit seemed ample, as we had planned, and the cabin space entirely adequate. Side decks of 16 inches seemed quite wide enough and to leave plenty of cabin space below. She seemed to be in every way just what we wanted.

Fitting a floor timber. The bilge clamp crosses the top of the picture.

We did insist on a fore hatch. This was partly to serve as an escape from the cabin. A fire in the galley or in the engine space could make it impossible to get through the main hatch. Even without a disaster, a fore hatch is important for anchor work. It is possible, people tell me, to put anchor chain down through a pipe in the deck into the space below. Of course some unfortunate soul, never the skipper of course, must creep forward over the bunks and spread out the wet chain as it comes down so it doesn't pile up under the pipe. If one uses rope, as I do, then said unfortunate must coil down the wet rope. Having been well acquainted with rope and chain for many years, I know that rope kinks and chain jams.

I remember a few busy moments in Menemsha, which I entered as paid skipper of a 37-foot yawl. In those ancient days there was room to anchor in Menemsha. As we edged in before the wind toward the beach, I dropped anchor and paid out scope, the chain snaking up out of its hole. It jammed. The yawl swung broadside to the wind and dragged her anchor toward the beach. I rushed below, found a link of chain jammed under the bilge clamp, yanked it clear, and got back on deck again in time to snub up the chain. The anchor bit in properly, the yawl swung into the wind with her stern in easy swimming distance—almost wading distance—from the beach, and all was well. But we were going to have a fore hatch.

Home we went, the decisions made, with everything going our way and spring rushing toward summer with giant steps.

Deck clamps, bilge clamps, and floor timbers in place.

# XI

## THE CRASH

THE FOLLOWING WEDNESDAY, APRIL 23, WE WENT TO the YMCA pool for our usual "keep-in-shape" swim. Mary had had a bad night, hurt badly from arthritis and other as-yet-undiagnosed ills, and hoped the swim would help. I felt great.

On the first lap, I was hit in the chest, hard. I walked to the shallow end and knew something was seriously wrong. Nevertheless, I dressed and Mary drove me to the hospital. Thanks to a good call by the doctor in charge, I was on my way to the Maine Medical Center in Portland by ambulance. I had suffered an aneurysm of the aorta, a serious affliction. Doctors Donegan, Kramer, and Aberjailey performed miracles of surgical replumbing about which I was scarcely aware.

Lying flat on my back in the hospital, entangled like a fly in a spiderweb of tubes and wires, I saw our whole life had crashed. Schooner, Friendship Sloop yearbook, magazine article, church responsibilities, woodpile, everything. I couldn't help Mary in her distress or even change a light bulb. I was helpless and useless. Mary wrote:

### The Day the Dam Broke

The day the dam broke
All was swept before it,
Including bits of our humanity,

Clinging to the broken bits of home.
On what strange shores
Will we be finally left?
Can we then pick up the pieces
Of you and me
And build once more a life
With bits of both the old and new?
Let's see what we can do.

THIS BEAT ALL the tubes and needles, although doctors, nurses, and hospital people were efficient, kind, and pleasant. Family and friends rallied around and brought encouragement, confidence, and help. My brother undertook to finish editing the Friendship Sloop yearbook, bringing computer-generated order into the confusion I had left. The editor of *Maine Boats & Harbors* extended the deadline on an article I had agreed to write. By May 2 I was in the rehabilitation hospital, able to sit up and write it. My church responsibilities I had fortunately left in good order, and the committee of which I was chairman carried on. *Dorothy Elizabeth* was planked up and deck framing was proceeding.

When, as a boy, I went cruising with my father, he would sometimes roust me out into the windy dark of a rough night for "anchor exercise." With our pajamas flapping about our legs, we would get the 60-pound anchor over the bow. I would maneuver the skiff under the anchor in the growing chop and row it out straight to windward as far as our heaviest rode would reach, then tip the anchor overboard. He took a strain on the line and made it fast around the mast. Then back to the warm bunk while the big anchor bit deep into the hard clay bottom. We slept, secure with an anchor to windward.

Damaged as I was, I had an anchor to windward. Mary, despite her afflictions, stood by with courage and confidence and made the hard decisions. My brother and sisters, my sons and grandsons, brought or sent support to both of us. Many friends came in to visit as I gained strength in the rehabilitation hospital, and a great many more sent cards. Many people prayed for me. I am convinced that good wishes sincerely felt, whether actually expressed or not, whether the sufferer is aware of them or not, help significantly in physical recovery. I don't understand it, but I know it.

> Old friends run deep
> In channels under ground
> And surface in the dry
> And barren land.
> Where I fell flat and thirsted
> They cool me in the sand.
>
> —MCD

## This is the way Ralph saw it:

ROGER CAME TO CHECK out the boat a week or so after the planking-up party, and some time after that I had a question for Roger. I don't know what it was—perhaps a question about the bridge deck. At any rate, I phoned and Mary answered. She was pretty flustered and said Roger was in the hospital. She couldn't tell me exactly what was wrong, but I gathered it was serious.

Well! This was a shock. What to do? I needed Roger's input. Although he was not working in the shop with us, he was still part of the team building the boat. Knowing that Roger and Mary were going to sail this boat was our inspiration to build this boat and do it right. What would we do without Roger?

As soon as possible, I called again and found out just what Roger had and that the operation was successful, although there were complications. I got Roger's phone number at the hospital and called. His voice sounded pretty feeble, but when we spoke of the boat, there seemed to be a spark of strength. Each time I called, his voice seemed stronger, and it was as if the boat encouraged him to keep going. We must keep working on the boat. I don't think there was ever a question of stopping work.

It was a great day when Roger and Mary finally came to the shop and climbed aboard the boat.

# XII

## BACK TO THE SCHOONER

AS SOON AS IT BECAME EVIDENT THAT I WAS NOT GOING to die, we decided that Ralph must go on with the schooner. It was obvious that I was not going to be able to finish her from a bare hull, at least not for too long a time. My left foot was paralyzed, and I was still very weak. Ralph would have to install the steering gear, which I had ordered from Lunenburg, as well as the engine, shaft, and stern bearing. Also, Ralph would have to install a fuel tank and get the engine running, for I had not the least idea of how to operate a diesel engine. All this, of course, would put off the delivery date into the fall, for besides working on *Dorothy Elizabeth*, Ralph and his crew would be very busy launching and fitting out yachts stored in his yard for owners who would want them right away yesterday or the day before.

Ralph called frequently with encouragement and with questions. Would I need bitts, or would a notch in the heel of the bowsprit suffice to hold the mooring line? Not at all. We needed a proper bitt to go down through the deck and step on the keel or a floor timber. There might be heavy strains on it, and they might come from many different directions. And we would need quarter bitts too. Sometimes we come alongside a float a little too fast and have to snub her up hard. A jibsheet cleat just will not stand the strain, and I bent the main traveler in the old *Dorothy* trying to tow someone. One can make significant decisions even while undergoing therapies.

Answering Ralph's questions helped a great deal in making me feel a part of building the vessel. The doctors, nurses, and therapists got interested in the progress of *Dorothy Elizabeth* too. I really believe I became to them a real person in a real world and not just another "patient," a specimen under a bell jar. That was the best therapy they could give me.

By April 29 Ralph reported to Mary that the floor timbers were in, the outside of the planking planed down, and the false frames for the chainplates in. Some builders bolt the chainplates through a plank and a timber and let it go at that. The chainplate takes the heavy strain of the shroud. If bolted only through a plank and a single timber, after a few years the side of the boat

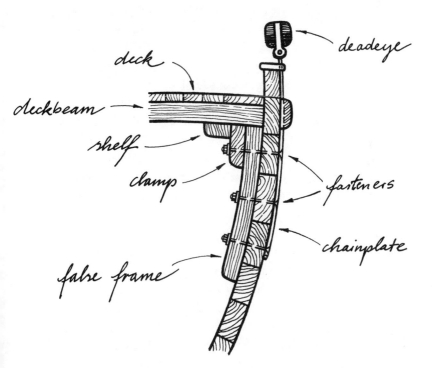

abreast the rigging develops a lift and is inclined to leak. It is reported that hard-driven fishing schooners opened up abreast the weather rigging so you could see light through the top seams. Ralph bolted the chainplates through a piece of oak that lay against the inside of the planking and had a lip to catch under the deck clamp, thus spreading the strain along the length of the boat.

By the first of May, the vessel was nearly caulked. Caulking is a skilled trade. It is more than just stuffing cotton into the space between the planks to keep Old Ocean out. When *Eastward* needed a seam recaulked, I bought a caulking iron, some cotton, and white lead, crawled underneath, and began to beat the cotton into the seam with a hammer. Someone who knew much more than I did stopped me short, took away the hammer, and borrowed a caulking mallet from the yard where we were hauled. A caulking mallet is a specialized tool. The head is about 15 inches long and of hardwood bound with iron every few inches. The cotton comes in a long, loose strand about ¾ inch in diameter. My outraged mentor tucked the strand of cotton into the seam in loose loops; then, starting at one end, he walked the iron along the seam, driving the cotton down evenly. He could tell when it was driven down properly by the sound the mallet made on the iron. It tunked on the first stroke and sounded a solid whack when the cotton was home. It is important to get the cotton even and tight because the caulking forces the planks against each other and thus makes the skin of the boat uniform and imparts a stiffness to the whole structure. The seam is made watertight by painting over the cotton and then paying the seam, filling the seam on top of the cotton with white lead or seam compound.

Caulking is a trade by itself, distinct from planking or timbering or rigging. In the days when all vessels were built of wood, gangs of caulkers would go from yard to yard caulking one vessel after another and doing nothing else. In Boston, at the

Richard caulking

time of the Revolution, they were so tightly organized and so politically influential that a political assembly became known as a caucus and still is. The *Oxford English Dictionary* gives this derivation but doubts its authenticity. Nevertheless, caulking is a trade, and caulkers are likely to be of independent mind. Richard is a good caulker. You get to thinking about these things after a month in the antiseptic atmosphere of a hospital.

However, a great deal was being done to relieve that antiseptic atmosphere. My brother, Donald, had picked up the end of that last plank when Andrea had sawed it off. On it he mounted a picture of her sawing it off. We hung it on the doorknob of my room and we explained it to every visitor. My cousin, also a saltwater man, brought six mats woven of nylon rope to be put under the ends of travelers on main-, fore-, and staysail sheets to prevent the sheet blocks from beating themselves to death on the deck. His young daughters brought brightly colored marine drawings we taped to the pale green walls. Our niece, my personal reflexologist, came in frequently, ministered to my paralyzed left foot, and brought strawberries to sparkle up hospital food.

Next, the question of portlights arose. How many should they be and of what material? We studied catalogues. Hard plastic was said to be light, durable, strong, and comparatively inexpensive. Aluminum is light and inexpensive. Bronze is heavy, strong, durable, expensive, and has an authority lacking in the others. I really don't like plastic. We had aluminum portlights in *Eastward*, and they corroded and leaked. I remembered that back in March I had seen bronze fittings at the Maine Boatbuilders Show in that cave under the eaves. Mary brought into our sanitized atmosphere the business-like catalogue of Traditional Marine Outfitters and in it we found bronze portlights for less than the glossy catalogues listed plastic. We called the telephone number listed and got Portland Yacht Services—not what we wanted at all. Donald, impetuous and indefatigable, went to 58 Fore Street and found Portland Yacht Services but no sign of Traditional Marine Outfitters. He pushed on into the office, a conventional civilized business office, and inquired of a coat-and-tie salesman for bronze portlights.

The atmosphere changed.

"Oh, you will have to see J. J. He's around here somewhere. His car's in the alley. Try the next building." He let Don out the back door into the alley, where stood a red car with a used look. He pushed open the door opposite, called out, but got no answer. Up a rough staircase he found an ill-lighted unfinished room under the eaves, and there stood J. J., bearded, uncombed, with long hair down his back. Don inquired for bronze portlights #01105PBZ.

"I think I got one o' them," said J. J. cheerfully and turned to shelves of bow chocks, stern lights, deck irons, ventilators. . . . With no hesitation, he pulled out a #01105PBZ portlight. Don explained that we were building a schooner and that the owner, his brother, was in the hospital and would like to see it before he bought it. J. J., again without hesitation, put it in Don's hands and bid him take it up to the hospital and come back with the answer. Nothing to sign, no down payment, no credit card number—complete trust and confidence.

Don brought it into the hospital room. It was too heavy for me to lift at the time, but it closed with a convincing clash; the dogs set the lid down tight on the gasket. It was real, solid, something from the world outside, a world that I missed among the white sheets and the wheelchairs. I sent him back to buy three more.

Back to Traditional Marine Outfitters. J. J. had no more but would order them and call. He gave Don his home telephone number in case he didn't get to calling. A week later, Mary called the number, heard J. J.'s friendly "Hello" with a background of many children's voices. He had the portlights; Don could pick them up in Portland. The next day he took a signed blank check to J. J.'s cave and in due course delivered the portlights to Ralph.

An old friend, Gail, who as a girl had raced Turnabouts with our boys at the Southport Yacht Club, drove all the way to Southwest Harbor to take pictures of *Dorothy Elizabeth* as she stood in the shop, deck framing going in, the engine hanging by a chain fall over the cockpit, waiting for the completion of the engine beds.

Meanwhile, at home, Don was overhauling gear for the float, which must be launched before son Bob and grandson Alec could bring *Eastward* around from the yard. As the whole world cranked up for summer, that day was coming soon. I received frequent bulletins, for Mary drove all the way from home to the hospital every day in spite of her own hurts. Don overhauled the chains that held the float to the shore. I missed the smell of the winter-dried weeds and mussels that he wire-brushed off and the mixture of tar, linseed oil, and turpentine with which he saturated the servings on the splices.

Nylon rope is quite elastic; it stretches. This is one of its virtues, for it absorbs sudden strains. However, an eye splice around a thimble can stretch enough to let the rope jump the thimble and chafe against the fitting around which it is spliced. We once found two strands of our dory painter chafed through after a rough day and night at sea. The solution is to splice the line a bit loosely around the thimble and put a good strain on it with a come-along. Then, with the nylon stretched, serve up the splice, pulling the marline tight enough with the mallet to pinch the nylon rope together right up to the thimble. The nylon, thus stretched, will lie against the thimble as hard as iron. Saturate the marline with tar to preserve it and—there you go.

The report that Mary had scraped last year's weeds off the float and that our neighbor Frank Luke and the men from his boatyard had painted and launched it disposed of that problem summarily.

Ordinarily, launching the float had been quite a project for Mary and me. On one of the first decent days in the spring, I had crawled underneath it when it lay on steeply inclined skids, and with putty knife and wire brush cleaned off the accumulated growth of weed, mussels, and barnacles from last year. Enough for one afternoon. Then, the day before launching, with roller and brush I painted the underneath of it with copper paint. This requires being clothed and gloved from head to foot with old clothes and equipped with protective glasses. I got a drop of copper paint in my eye once. I told the doctor,

"It hurts like hell!" He told me that copper paint does contain irritating oils. Two ways of saying the same thing.

At low water on launching day we grease the skids with kitchen grease saved up during the winter. As the tide comes, we drag the peapod down the hill and onto the float. When the tide is up to the lower ends of the skids, we pass a pinch line from a tree to an iron on the float, which will hold the gangway later. Then I lean precariously over the lower end of the float with a wrecking bar and pull the nails that all winter have held the float from sliding down.

We are ready to go. The peapod is on the float. Mary is on the float tending a line to the wharf. I am on the float, holding a turn on the pinch line—and we don't go. She sticks. I jump up and down to start her, but she doesn't start. So I make fast the pinch line, get off the float, and, with a pry, jiggle her a bit. She starts, fetches up against the pinch line. I leap aboard again and slack the pinch line a little. She starts, she goes, she zips the pinch line out of my hands, rushes down the skids, and plunges into the coming tide. For the first time in the coming season, we are afloat. Piloting a walker down the polished hall, I miss it.

On May 8, Mary, Don, and Joyce went to Rockland to read

proof on the Friendship Sloop yearbook and on to Southwest Harbor to take pictures. They reported the deck laid and caulked, the bulkhead between engine and cabin in place, engine on its beds, steering gear bolted down. Spring was fast spilling into summer, and on June 12, seven weeks after the crash, I was released from the hospital and, rather shakily, came home.

# XIII

## *EASTWARD*

THE SUMMER SLIPPED BY, MOST OF IT DEDICATED TO therapy for my paralyzed left foot and to regaining strength. Exercises prescribed by my demanding therapist at home and in the YMCA swimming pool occupied much of the day. Sitting in a chair on the porch and pushing a walker about the house and yard occupied most of what remained. However, there were memorable experiences.

You will remember that we had given our Friendship sloop *Eastward* to our son, Bob. He planned to sail parties in her, as we had, with his son Alec as skipper. Alec, who was about to start college, would have summers available, but although he had served frequently as mate on *Eastward* and for all the previous summer had cruised with us, lived aboard, and done much of the navigating, he had not enough days of service to qualify for his Coast Guard license to carry passengers for hire. Therefore, he was to go as skipper every possible day during the summer of 1997 and take guests without pay as often as possible—this to oblige any of our old customers and to keep *Eastward* in the public eye in anticipation of 1998 when he could expect to have his license. Bob would go as mate whenever he could, which would be often.

Accordingly, on June 13, when Alec had graduated from high school and Bob had wound up his responsibilities as assistant headmaster for the school year, they got right to work fitting out

*Eastward* as she lay afloat at the C&B yard. They had already sanded and painted the spars as they lay on horses in the big shed. They at once laid out the rigging in our garage, repaired and painted the servings on the standing rigging, knocked the pins out of the blocks, cleaned and greased the sheaves, and painted the blocks. Mary and I had always done this ourselves on a pleasant June day when the blackflies weren't too fierce. Now I stumped out to the garage, pushing the walker, and watched with interest.

By June 20 they had hung the rigging on the mast and stepped it. I stopped by the yard to inspect. It was difficult to navigate the walker down the gangway and along the float, but I did it and actually sat on the deck for a bit. To see the spars in place, the rigging set up, all shining in new paint, and to feel the slight motion of a floating boat under me was a stirring experience and one that did me nothing but good.

On June 23 they brought *Eastward* around to her mooring off our house. We had owned *Eastward* for 41 years, but I had almost never seen her under sail, for not in all that time had she left her mooring without me aboard. Of course I had seen many photographs and several paintings. Once on a gentle day I had left Mary aboard at the wheel and rowed off in the peapod to take a picture. She was a lovely sight, but she seemed to be scarcely moving. A little air came in before I could get aboard and Mary, overcome by the feeling of complete independence that the singlehander feels, squared away for foreign ports. I rowed as hard as ever I have rowed in a race but could not gain. *Eastward* glided ahead of me imperturbably over a silky sea. At last Mary relented, slacked sheets, and let me back aboard, but I have been reluctant to repeat the performance.

Now, however, shore-bound by doctor's orders, I pushed my limits, tottered halfway down to the shore to watch her come up the bay before a good breeze. She was powerful. She

*Eastward*

was stately. She was regal. She was magnificent. A photograph, even a movie, cannot convey the whole scene: the feel of the wind, the smell of rockweed, the vessel moving, alive, through living water in a living world of trees, rocks, islands, among gulls and seals and terns. The bone in her teeth is not a frozen patch of white on paper but a foaming wave ever renewed under her bow, ever flowing back along her side. I choked down the thrill to coach Alec soundlessly as he brought her alongside the float.

"Too fast! Too fast! Swing her off and try again." Alec agreed, I guess, because that is what he did.

"Again too fast." But this time, as she swung by close to the float, the mainsheet, hanging slack, caught the bitt on the corner of the float and fetched her up all standing. Bob on the foredeck got a line ashore. Nothing parted and all was well. Thus we learn at every age.

I had other chances to watch *Eastward* under way during the summer, but never again was I so moved. In August, when my medical advisor allowed me to sail at last, I made my walker way determinedly down the steep path to the wharf without even thinking how I was to get up again; and helped by Bob and Alec, got aboard. Everything was just as it always had been. The reef points pattered on the mainsail; the jaws of the boom squeaked on the mast. We cast off. Bob hoisted the staysail as he always had. But it was different, for I was a passenger. I was watching, not doing. Alec at the wheel trimmed the mainsheet and bore off, intent on not running down the peapod bobbing at the mooring. I was soon given the wheel, and again it felt perfectly natural, just as it always had. The littlest tremble in the luff of the mainsail flattening out into a full sail, bubbles going by the lee rail, sound of wind in taut wire, taut rope, taut canvas. It was breathlessly familiar, yet so different. I had been ashore so long. It wasn't my boat. I didn't even have a boat except the idea of a boat down in Southwest Harbor, and I almost doubted her reality as a living, moving vessel.

I was invited to go several other times in 1997. One of the best was the last, the day Bob and Alec took *Eastward* back to the C&B yard to lay up for the winter. It was a lovely late August day, August because schools and colleges now open barbarically early. We sailed farther than we needed, stretched the afternoon. Bob reminded me of the day he had sailed my father's schooner *Dorothy* to the yard on another last day. He had for crew a classmate of my father's, a cruising companion in earlier years, married to a lady who preferred antiquing to sailing. She had agreed to meet them at the yard at 4:30. About 3:45 Bob had said it was time to head for the yard if they were to be on time.

"A woman can get only so mad. Let's stay out another hour."

Today Alec planned to land under sail at the yard as usual, but the tide runs hard and the wind is fluky up among the wharves. The sail filled at the wrong moment and *Eastward* picked up speed. Alec swung off. The tide was setting him down on a moored yacht, but he squeaked by without hitting her to try again. This time, allowing for the fluky wind and the tide, he made it neatly. We were all sinfully proud of him.

In two days they had taken ashore everything that would move, bagged the sails and hung them in the garage, and were gone. Their summer was over but not ours. *Eastward*, without her mast, lay under a cover in a slip, afloat until cold weather.

ANOTHER DAY, a year later. By this time Alec had earned his license as captain and was regularly carrying passengers with his father as mate, and I had discarded walker and cane.

"Hey, Cap," Alec asked, "Could you go mate with me today? Dad's away." What an offer! The old guy with a game leg being asked by the Captain to go mate!

"I'd be delighted." We were to take my cousin, Stefan Bader, and his 18-month-old daughter, Natasha. It was a lovely August day with a pleasant westerly breeze. Alec hoisted the mainsail just as I used to when I was skipper. I knew I hadn't the strength to do it now, but I found I could get around the foredeck pretty smartly. Between us we set the topsail. I remembered the drill and found all the lines belayed where they had always been. Alec took the wheel. I dropped the mooring on order, hoisted the staysail and then the jib, coiled down halyards, and picked up the fenders over the side. Then there wasn't much for the mate to do but tend jibsheets when we tacked and play with Natasha.

She was a delightful little round-faced blonde with a built-in grin. She had been so well brought up that she had never been frightened and never met anyone who didn't love her. Pulling off someone else's hat was her idea of the funniest thing she had ever done.

Alec let me steer for a while. That was fun too.

About 3 miles from home, I noticed clouds building up to the westward, looking a little like young thunderheads. They were a long way off still, and often storms over the land go by to the north of us. Still, they were there and slowly rising. Nothing to worry about. Alec was watching them too, and he was the skipper. I kept on not saying anything.

About 10 minutes after I would have headed for home, Alec up-helmed and allowed it was about time. The squall appeared to be working to the north and didn't look very savage anyway, but it was time to run. I had seen all the snappy thunderstorms I needed.

As we crossed the bay toward home, the squall was clearly going north of us, but we would likely get the edge of it. The cloud covered the sun, and we could see a line of wind coming across the water. Alec gave me the wheel and went forward to take in the topsail. He had just got it down, when the wind struck and gave him a hard time collecting the flapping slatting sail, but he did it just as the rain struck. We were almost home. The wind was brisk, and we were tearing along ahead of it in the rain toward a lee shore. As Alec shoved the topsail down the hatch out of the way, he asked,

"Can you shoot the mooring?"

"I've done it before," I answered. What else could I say? It had been a long time since I had made a mooring, a long time since I had had to make any decision on a boat. I had done it before, but I had missed moorings before. If I missed, I figured between us we could probably get *Eastward* under control again before we went ashore, but it could deteriorate into a very unpleasant situation. Probably, though, no one would get hurt. So what could I say?

"I've done it before."

Rain was running out from under Natasha's blonde hair into her laughing eyes as she reached for my hat.

"I've done it before."

We bore down on the buoy with the peapod tailing off from it, leaving it what I judged to be the right distance to port.

"Dump the staysail, Alec." Down it came—halfway. The downhaul parted. As I rounded up, the flapping sail got in Alec's way, but we ranged up alongside the peapod about right. Alec fought his way from under the sail, picked up the buoy handily, made fast and dropped the mainsail. Natasha, with the rain running into her eyes, was still laughing.

As we rowed ashore, "Good day, Cap; thanks a lot," said Alec.

"Thank you, Cap. My pleasure."

## As Alec Saw It:

WITH DAD OUT OF TOWN and family visiting from Massachusetts, I decided I would sail *Eastward* up into Boothbay to show the flag. With Dad absent I would take family as crew and passengers. I asked Grampy, now 16 months from the Crash, to go mate and, as I did when he used to ask me, he jumped at the chance. Once on board he joked, "I sure hope I remember where everything goes." Some things you won't ever forget.

Our passengers were my dad's cousin Stefan and daughter, Natasha, of about 18 months going out for her first sail. Natasha was and still is 20 pounds of cute in a 10 pound bag. Because the wind was from the northwest, I rowed ashore to ferry people out instead of messing around with a downwind staysail landing. As I rowed toward the dock, I lifted my head to see *Eastward*; mainsail and topsail set pointing to the wind. But what made me stop rowing for a second was my grandfather. Leaning on the coaming, mainsheet in one hand and twiddling the spokes with the other. His cane gone and bad leg not visible, he looked as at home as I had seen him since the Crash.

Stefan and I passed Natasha into the skiff like a picnic basket, then packaged her in a life jacket that was more than a bit too big for her. As I rowed, her blonde hair, blue eyes, and big smile seemed to reflect my blond hair, blue eyes, and big smile like a funhouse mirror. Once aboard and under way I gave Grampy the wheel and played with Natasha. In fact, we all took turns steering and playing with Natasha. As she played with Grampy's hat I noticed through my sunglasses that the sky was getting darker to the northwest. I took a confirming peek from under my sunglasses just to be sure, and it was darkening. It wasn't *too* black, so we kept going toward the flasher off Tumbler Island. Grampy and I were both watching the clouds, and I am sure he would have turned around before I decided to. Live and learn. It began to get pretty dark up above, and we were going to get rained on; that was apparent. We made it around Spruce Point, and for a brief minute it looked like we might make it. We heard thunder roll behind us, but I did not take the topsoil in. I wanted to be home as fast as possible. Seconds after the thunder, the wind and lots of it. I told Grampy to steer, and I hopped up the wet deck to take in the topsail. I had waited to take it in until it was blowing too hard, and now it was blowing too hard. As much as I wrestled and fought that sail, it fought and wrestled me back. I was on the lee side with my feet braced against the main rigging, ankle-deep in the water that was rushing over the bow. I fought it down and pitched the now-silent ball of canvas down the hatch.

I looked at the situation I had put myself in. A thunder squall with high winds, rain, and a lee shore behind our mooring. My crew was capable, but not sure-footed on the slippery foredeck. Knowing that as captain I was responsible for all that happened, both good and bad, do I take the wheel and put him as close to being on top of the mooring as possible and risk his slipping on the wet, uneven deck? Or do I take the deck and let him sail me to the mooring, risking that he misses and we fall off on the lee shore? That is a hell of a choice to have to make. Having seen Grampy do this many times before, I asked him from the foredeck, "You think you can shoot that mooring?" He looked back at me and said he'd do his best.

As we went for the mooring and I dumped the staysail, the downhaul parted. I stood on the stem and tried to paw it down. It fought back too, trying to climb the stay and grab every breath of wind it could. It finally came down just in time for me to grab the boathook and reach over the bow, gaff up the pennant, and slide the loop over the bit. Grampy and I met at the halyards and dumped the mainsail. Thank God, I thought. Needless to say, Natasha had a whale of an introduction to sailing, but despite all the rain she laughed and smiled all the way home.

Later in the summer, with Dad away once again and my cousin Mark as mate and an engine that would not start, I saw dark clouds, headed for home early, and took in sail early, and not one of the passengers got wet. So I continue to learn. My library of stories continues to grow, hopefully not too large.

# XIV

## HOMECOMING

OTHER GOOD THINGS HAPPENED DURING THE SUMMER of '97. On July 3, Bob and Alec helped me downstairs to the shop, and eagerly shoved furniture and boxes out of the way to clear a path for me and my walker to the bench, where I confronted the splice I had left on April 22 with its six strands sticking out stiffly in six different directions. I picked up the marlinespike from where I had set it down when Mary had called me to dinner that day, wondering whether I now had the strength to force it under a strand. On this possibly the whole future of *Dorothy Elizabeth* depended. I did it. I slid the spike in, ran it up the wire, tucked the strand, ran it back to its place, and cut it in as I always had. It was, in a small way, a great triumph. My physical body was working again. I was in control, moving toward launching and toward sailing. I finished that splice and served it up. Now I forget which splice it was, but it ought to glow in the dark.

During the summer, fall, and winter, I went on with the rigging, making tighter and smoother splices and doing them more quickly. On April 4, 1998, I finished the last one.

Several other beacons flash back to me from that summer. The Maine post of the Cruising Club of America, of which I was recently post captain, had planned before the Crash a gam at Luke's boatyard for June 21, to inspect and celebrate *Dorothy Elizabeth*. Of course she would not be there, but they planned to come anyway. Only a week home from the hospital, I doubted if

I could make it; but I gathered up what strength I had, and with my trusty walker got down on the wharf, sat on a box in the sun, and talked with a number of good friends who had sailed over big oceans. Frank Luke saw that I got safely from car to wharf and back, undamaged. This was another reassuring contact with the real world.

Among many visitors:

Brad Simmons, near neighbor, came to set out moorings and sat on the porch while I explained how I had left them last fall. Fred McIntyre, water commissioner, had heard that I was dead and came by to be reassured to the contrary and to tell me how he had been afflicted.

Bob and Barbara Ireland picked up our guest mooring in their sloop *Roving Kind*. Bob had been superintendent of schools in Concord, Massachusetts, when I was chairman of the School Committee. He and Barbara stopped by every summer to bring me and *The Cruising Guide* to the *New England Coast* up to date on harbors they had visited.

A strange little sloop flying a Canadian flag picked up our guest mooring. Up the bank came an agile little man using two canes. He had met *Eastward* in Pulpit Harbor and asked Bob to sign his copy of the *Guide*, and Bob invited him to use our guest mooring. Both his feet were paralyzed in a motorcycle accident some years before, but he had not let that slow him up. He was cruising west from Halifax alone, had in mind to visit Portland, and wondered whether it was worthwhile to go west of that. He was such an exciting man that we offered him a ride to the store, a shower, a drink, and dinner—all of which he accepted with enthusiasm. He departed early in the morning, leaving on our porch the flashlight he had borrowed the night before and a copy of *Ice* by Tristan Jones. Jones had lost a leg, but he had rebuilt an old lifeboat, sailed from England to Iceland, wintered on the east coast of Greenland, was frozen into pack ice for another year, and finally landed on Spitsbergen, Norway. Since then he has sailed small boats in many latitudes and written at least 15 books. Remarkable what a man can do with one leg!

Another visitor came from Germany with his wife and small daughter to look at *Eastward*. He said there was a market for wooden boats in Europe and the Caribbean because with the increase in fiberglass, aluminum, and steel boats, no one in Europe knew how to build wooden boats anymore, "except a few old duffers over 80, and they're no good." At any boat show, he said, people walk by the state-of-the-art production yachts with their hands in their pockets, but they cluster around wooden boats. They want to be near them, to touch them. I was able to tell him that our neighbor Tim Hodgdon was building a 124-foot wooden sloop for an Italian, that Ralph Stanley had just built a sloop for a lady in Sardinia and was then building a Friendship sloop for an Englishman. And, of course, there is *Dorothy Elizabeth*.

Other people stopped by for tea or a glass on our porch. My cousin and coauthor of the *Guide*, Wally Fenn, and his wife, Carol, visited for a day, and the commodore of the Cruising Club of America picked up our mooring and came ashore. These cheered and encouraged me no little.

A most welcome visitor was my old shipmate Hugh Williams. We had grown up together during summers in New Harbor, splashed about in punts, learned to sail in dories and skiffs, and leaped with shouts of laughter into the cold waters of the harbor. Later he had a 24-foot Muscongus Bay sloop, and I sailed my father's 28-foot sloop *Dorothy*. In college we established Apprentice Cruises with a house flag bearing our initials, D&W, often interpreted Dead to Windward. He had a 26-foot sloop by this time. We took five boys cruising, teaching them how to have a good time safely at sea. We have been allies in a number of projects since.

As we received reports from Ralph's shop of the continuing progress on *Dorothy Elizabeth*, I visited Frank Luke's yard in late

July, hoping that he could still find a place to lay out her spars and to set her up so I could work on her. To my delight, Frank was eager to have her, would step her masts, launch her, and store her under cover for the winter where I could get at her. If I wanted to get aboard, he volunteered to lash a chair to his bucket loader and set me down on deck.

One morning, between sleep and waking, I had frightful doubts as to whether I had made the springstay between the mastheads 8′ 9″ or 9′ 8″. Before breakfast, I checked and measured. I was right. It was 8′ 9″.

Ralph called several times in the first week of August asking for decisions: How high should the wheel box be? How much clearance did I want between the box and the wheel? How high should be the seats beside the wheel? How high should he make the toerail? We could not possibly make these decisions without seeing the boat. As the doctor's prohibition against driving long distances had expired, we drove to Southwest Harbor on August 8.

We climbed aboard up steps and a staging Ralph had rigged for us, and sat in the cockpit for a while to get the feel of her. She was still far from finished, but she looked right and felt right. Looking forward, with no top yet on the house, we admired again her easy entrance folding into a flat run. The cockpit was entirely adequate, nearly as big as *Eastward*'s and deep enough to feel secure even without coamings. We were concerned about the flush hatch over the engine. If it was tight enough to keep it from leaking, it would swell when wet to be so tight I could not get it off. As it turned out, the concern was legitimate. We had little trouble settling the height of the seat by the wheel—14 inches—and the toerail—2¼ inches, with a cap.

The cabin would have nearly full headroom. It makes little sense to me to spoil the looks of a boat by building a high house so a tall man can stand up straight. We are short people, and we can scrooch a little or sit down. There appeared to be room enough for a galley, a chart table, a head, and two bunks, but we decided to make no decisions on the cabin. The first priority was to get this schooner under sail.

It gave us both a great lift to see her again, for in spite of photographs and reports by visiting friends, she seemed to exist only in our imagination. To see her, to go aboard, to sit in the cockpit, was another long step toward the reality from which we had been snatched in April.

Ralph was to bring the spars down to Frank's on Labor Day weekend but decided that was no time to be on Route 1 with 30-foot spars on a pickup truck. However, on September 19, he brought them down. They appeared to be quite light and limber after *Eastward*'s massive mainmast but were as specified. They were of tough island spruce, cut on Deer Isle, and although sealed with thinned varnish, the masts had several wide and long checks. These are cracks running along the grain where the wood dries on the outside before it dries on the inside. The outside shrinks and pulls open. The checks don't do any real harm, and commercial builders used to ignore them. It is possible, however, that water could collect in a check and start a pocket of rot, and anyway, checks are unsightly. Ralph said to pour hot beeswax into them. The wax is flexible enough to come and go as the wood swells and shrinks, and paint will hold on it. He thought we would need about 5 pounds. That, it turned out, is a lot of beeswax.

With the spars actually within 150 yards of our house, I felt that there was not a moment to lose. We must get those spars ready for the rigging, even if the rigging was far from ready. Accordingly, on September 23 we headed upcountry for the home of Melanie Dumont in Windsor, Maine. She is deeply committed to bees, honey, and beeswax. She collects combs from beekeepers for miles around, strips the honey, and refines the wax. She sells considerable wax to Bath Iron Works for electronic work. She was so enthusiastic about bees that Mary asked her if she ever wrote poems about bees. She did not but immediately shifted intellectual gears and asked if Mary wrote poems. Mary recited:

> How I strived and strived to be
> What others tried to make of me,
> 'Till in a corner on a shelf,
> O joy, O joy, I found myself.
> I took me down, brushed off the dust.
> No more, no more myself shall rust.
> O jubilation, I am free
> Forevermore to be just me.

Melanie was delighted. Apparently that shoe fit perfectly. She insisted that Mary recite it slowly so she could write it down. Then, shifting gears again, she took Mary out to the barn to show her the honey operation. We came away with 5 pounds of wax and a new understanding of bees.

That same day we went along to Ralph's to see how he was getting on. We found Richard and a helper marking in the waterline—a fussy job. He established spots at the bow and stern where the waterline should come, set up a horizontal support at each end, and stretched a string fore and aft. Of course it touched the curved side of the boat at only one place, so Richard had a helper go ahead of him to push the string straight in against the side of the boat while Richard tapped in a nail about every 8 inches. Because the boat curves both up and down as well as fore and aft, the string tended to slide down. Richard had to sight along it constantly and keep the nails in line behind him, with the string ahead. This was a heavy strain on his equanimity, which occasionally cracked.

We scrambled aboard and found great changes. The house

was on, its top covered with canvas and painted with primer. The planking seams were all caulked and payed. Cockpit coamings were on, and the steering gear braced and bolted. The fuel tank was in but not fastened, and there was as yet no toerail or handrail on top of the house, so I was reluctant to creep forward on the narrow deck. Mary tried the fore hatch again and found it difficult, but she did it. As I sat on the wheel box with the whole boat in front of me—cockpit, cabin house, and foredeck—*Dorothy Elizabeth* felt about ready to go, ready to slide out of the shop and come home, ready to be rigged and to go to sea. I enjoyed this feeling briefly, and then I peered down the hatch at the engine.

I managed to trace the course of the saltwater cooling system through the heat exchanger, through a loop leading above the waterline to prevent siphoning, and back into the exhaust. I also traced the fuel line, but even with this profound knowledge, I had really no idea of what I would do if she overheated or refused to run. This bad situation I must remedy before we go to sea.

With more enthusiasm, we turned to a study of the rigging plan. A chilling discovery. A note: "turnbuckle not included." Did this mean that the measurements Ralph had given me were to the top of the turnbuckle or did not include an allowance for it? Have I made bobstay, forestay, and springstay too short? Will I have to buy more wire and do these over again? I will have to get home, remeasure, and see if I have made a stupid mistake.

With this cheery thought lurking in the back of my head, it was a long drive home after a long day. While Mary heated up the dinner casserole, I got the measurements from the file and found, "springstay 8′ 9″ including turnbuckle" and the same for forestay and bobstay. Shroud measurements were given "to chainplate." I had, then, done it correctly. With great relief, we enjoyed that casserole.

A busy but unproductive two weeks followed, of which the

outstanding event was my attempt to swat a fly on the kitchen window. I did it decisively, so decisively that I broke the window. Getting the sash and the aluminum runs out of the frame, setting new glass, and getting it all put back together again interrupted rigging work, but one moves slowly with only a leg and a half. Just as I finished with that miserable window, Nat Wilson came in to talk about sails.

When we had first decided to build *Dorothy Elizabeth*, Nat had agreed to make the sails, but being busy with *Constitution*'s topsails and other work, he had not started ours. Now that summer had slacked off into fall, he was ready. He brought with him a swatch of Oceanus sailcloth. It was Dacron, but quite unlike the hard, stiff, bright-white Dacron we were used to. This was as soft as cotton duck and of a pleasant off-white color. Nat had developed this cloth in concert with North Sails as a "cruising" sail to suit the owner who did not need the extreme stiffness and resistance to stretch of a racing sail, who did not like being blinded by staring at the luff on a bright day, and who would rather furl a sail than flake it down. We agreed at once that he should use it. He declared he would have no trouble taking the measurements off the sail plan Ralph had given us. Here was another step nearer going sailing.

Then Ralph called to say *Dorothy Elizabeth* was ready to come home. This involved some planning. We intended to bring her home over the road, for neither she nor I was ready to motor from Southwest Harbor in the short days of October with no sails or ballast aboard, with me dependent on a cane and utterly ignorant of a diesel engine. She would have to come down on a Brownell trailer, which is equipped with hydraulic arms to lift, support, and steady her, even at 50 miles per hour. But there is no way such a trailer can get into Ralph's shop to pick her up. Therefore she must be launched, towed across the harbor, and picked out of the water on the other side. We at length coordinated the tides, Ralph's schedule, the schedule of Charlie Jenness of the C&B Marina who owned the trailer, and Frank Luke, who was to receive her. It was all arranged for Thursday, October 16—including the insurance, which I very nearly forgot.

But there is always something to keep the bear's tail short. Charlie called on Wednesday to say that his trailer could not go into the water far enough to lift out a boat that drew as much as ours because he had no winch on the trailer that could haul it out again. A call in distress to Ralph put him to seeking a solution. He called back to say that his friend Dan Chalmers had a trailer that could take out *Dorothy Elizabeth*. The proper thing to do, of course, was to have Dan take her all the way to East Boothbay, but having committed myself to Charlie and being of an inflexible mind, I didn't think of it. We arranged to have Dan pull her out and set her up in the parking lot on the shore, and have Charlie take her from there.

Thursday morning we left home at 6:30 for Southwest Harbor. *Dorothy Elizabeth* had been slid down the ways in a ballasted cradle at low water and was scheduled to float off at 9:30. This was not the "official" launching. We agreed not to count it. Nevertheless, we wanted to be there.

We didn't make it. We arrived at 9:15 to find that an unusually high tide had floated her off about 9:00, and she was lying alongside the float. This was the first time we had seen her from far enough away to tell what she looked like. She was elegant, neat, all of a piece, not a combination of pieces. Yet she looked uncomfortable. Unballasted, she floated well above her designed waterline and rather down by the stern. She seemed to be crying out for attention, for someone to put her to rights.

Richard was not satisfied with her. There were still things to be done before he would let her go. The hole for the foremast was not quite round and not quite centered. He departed in a hurry and returned with a sanding drum, a portable drill, and

Bill Tefft

ABOVE: **Out of Ralph's shop.** OPPOSITE: **Down the ways.**

several batteries. While the drum growled and snarled at perfecting the mast hole, he sent one man for red lead to paint the insides of the mast steps and another for a cold chisel and a hammer to tighten the stuffing-box nut. Ralph had said he would drink whatever water she leaked crossing the harbor. He never wet his whistle.

About 11:00, after we had admired and enjoyed our new boat, Richard was more or less satisfied that she was fit to leave his care. Ralph came alongside in his lobster boat, *Seven Girls*, and we moved gently down the harbor.

Bill Tefft

She was afloat. She felt afloat with a gentle motion, a little more where the northwest wind got a fetch down Somes Sound. I took the wheel, although there wasn't much steering to do, as Ralph controlled our course from *Seven Girls*.

Too soon we were alongside another float from which I watched Dan Chalmers twitch her out of the water. Charlie was ready with his trailer to take her home.

We set off soon after, taking turns driving, eating peanut butter sandwiches, drinking ginger ale, and wondering whether we would catch up. We didn't.

When we rolled into Frank's yard, he and his crew were setting her up with her waterline horizontal so her bowsprit drew out her sheerline and she would look her best. Our cousins Douglas and Ruth Day, happily just arrived from Florida, were taking TV pictures of the busy scene. We stood around and admired our new boat for a while, but as there didn't seem to be anything constructive we could do, we went home to tea.

The Homecoming was celebrated by a party on Saturday for anyone interested in welcoming *Dorothy Elizabeth*. It wasn't a launching, but it was the next thing to it. I had written a piece for the paper, told all our friends at the Y, at church, at the Historical Society. Acquaintances met at the store or the post office who asked, "How's the new boat coming along, Cap?" Ralph and Marion came from Southwest Harbor, and Richard stopped by long enough to deliver the handrails for the top of the house and to fasten the chocks for the anchor rode on the bowsprit. Bob and Alec came from Massachusetts. Frank had a table set up on horses for us. His wife, Nora, and his mother, Verna, helped Mary and Cousin Ruth lay out cookies, cakes, beer, various colas, and soft drinks. My brother Donald added style to the occasion as he had at the shutter party with well-chosen selections on the pipes. *Dorothy Elizabeth*'s many friends welcomed her with a celebration worthy of her builder and the occasion.

# XV

## SUMMER'S OVER

### SUMMER'S OVER

The silver sunpath after Labor Day
Turns burnished pewter; sunset light grows pale.
Sea glitters steely blue or iron gray,
And heavy winds bear down the close-reefed sail.
Floats are hauled, the lonely wharves left bare.
Blue-covered yachts in side-yards huddle down.
Late blooming tourists photograph and stare
At scarlet trees and islands turning brown.
A northeast gale hurls gusts of rain to strip
The land for winter. Though faded leaves still try
To cling to August with a desperate grip,
It blows the last of summer from the sky.
Now come short days, warm hearts, nights cold and long.
Come book and pen, come needle, dance and song.

—RFD

SUMMER PEOPLE ASK US ON A WARM, SUNNY DAY IN August, "What do you do all winter?" One sharp-tongued local lady answered, "We put on our L. L. Bean caps, pull down the earflaps, sit on a stone wall, and wait for you to come back."

We are busy first in picking up after summer. Boatyards haul two or three or four yachts on every high tide. Shrink-wrapped yachts spiked with bare masts fill in their parking lots and back lots. Floats and gangways are hauled, leaving bare wharves and harbors punctuated with winter sticks.

Last year we had our parts in this ourselves. At high water we hauled our gangway onto our wharf with a come-along. Then, using our float as a working platform, we hauled our moorings up to the chains, again with the come-along, bent on the winter stick, and dropped the chains into the mud where they lay dormant all winter. At high water the next day, we hooked our four-wheel-drive car to the float and ran it up the skids above the highest tides. With float chains and mooring pennants hung in the shed and the peapod stowed under the porch, we were snugged down for the winter.

THIS PARTICULAR FALL, however, we were neither strong nor agile enough to face this annual challenge, so left it to Frank and his crew to haul the float and to Brad Simmons to deal with the moorings. We tended to storm windows, boardwalks, and the raking of leaves. *Dorothy Elizabeth*, now without her bowsprit, was tucked away in a shed, her spars in a rack.

On October 24 we were invited to visit Tim Hodgdon's shop, where he was building a 124-foot sloop for an Italian yachtsman. It filled the whole building. Back to the wall and nose against the planking, we found it hard to get any idea of her from the ground, but we could see the 106,000-pound lead keel. From a staging at deck height we could look down on her. She was luxury afloat, finished out in cherry wood with a fireplace it took two men two years to build. Her carbon-fibre mast will be 170 feet high. It is being built in New Zealand; and if Bath Iron Works cannot step it, she will be towed to Newport to have it done. She will draw 9 feet with the centerboard up and 26 feet with the board down. A captain and four men will run her with the help of numerous power winches and a bow thruster.

One can speculate on the relationship of size and expense to pleasure. My brother sold his 36-foot schooner and bought a little fiberglass Herreshoff sloop, claiming he could have 90 percent as much fun in 10 percent as much boat.

Reduce the size of the boat still further. We visited Tim Sherman's shop to see the half-model of *Eastward* he had built. It was a work of art, accurate and beautifully finished. He also had in his shop half-models of Cup defenders and several other vessels. He was a cabinetmaker by profession and found pleasure in half a boat built to the scale of half an inch to a foot.

*Dorothy Elizabeth* is little more than half done, and it has been more than a year since our visit to Ralph on our September cruise, but I have had my money's worth out of her already—in fact, I can't express our pleasure in her in terms of money. I hope the owner of a 124-foot sloop with a 170-foot mast and bow thrusters feels the same.

Our Florida cousin, Doug Day, is a skillful woodworker. The day after Homecoming he had been eager to get right to work on *Dorothy Elizabeth*. It appeared to us that a pair of gaff jaws would be the right place to start. He had brought his own tools.

We brought the fore gaff home and set it up in the shop. From the firewood pile I had saved several twisty pieces of oak that seemed to take the same natural bend the jaws might take. I took Doug to the yard where *Eastward*'s spars were stored, showed him her gaff, and explained what was needed. He went right at it while I stood out of his light, adjusted the band saw for the work he was doing, went to the store for bolts, hooked up the new motor for the table saw, and answered technical questions as well as I could. The chips flew, the saws howled and growled, and by suppertime I had two elegant gaff jaws.

However, the mast is about 5½ inches in diameter and the gaff only about 3½ inches. If the gaff were flattened to provide a good bearing for the jaws, they would be only about 2½ inches apart and would nowhere near fit around the mast. Doug exhumed from my scrap pile two pieces of oak and cut wedges to hold the jaws apart. Just then, we were called to the table. Doug and Ruth departed the next day, but at least we had made a start.

I went over to Frank's yard one day to talk with him about what had to be done this winter besides splicing rigging. We talked about it sitting in the cockpit; sitting in the cockpit was in itself a pleasure. He asked about a bilge pump. We certainly would need one because even if she leaked no more than Ralph could drink, rain and spray in the cockpit would drain right into the bilge. Should she ship a sea, a good bilge pump would be much in demand.

"Electric?" asked Frank.

Not at all. With my conviction, firmly based on experience, that mechanical gadgets are subject to failure on salt water, I wanted a simple, large-capacity, manual pump. The type we used to use, called a guinea pump, was simply a 4-inch galvanized stovepipe with a leather flapper valve on the bottom and a spout on the top. A stick with a cone of leather, point down, was the plunger. It was awkward to stow and exhausting to use, but it moved a lot of water and you didn't need to be a certificated engineer to fix it. Since then, technology has improved vastly on the guinea pump. Frank happened to have a big diaphragm pump by Edson, a simple thing as big as a soup tureen with two flapper valves and a diaphragm. It was comparatively easy to take apart in case of trouble and had enormous capacity. The handle would stick up through the cockpit floor and work fore and aft. Frank thought you could pump a pair of socks through it. He would see that it was installed to discharge through the counter.

My father's sloop, the original *Dorothy* built in 1925, had a very simple pump in her cockpit. One pulled up on a handle, and bilge water spurted out the side of the boat. My father was welcoming a classmate and his wife, who had just come alongside in a skiff. Their young son in the cockpit seized the handle of the pump, asking "What's this?" His mother in her summer dress got the answer.

On October 31, I stopped by the sail loft to see how Nat was coming on with the sails. To my surprise, they were nearly all done—only the topsail remained to be cut. Jinny was doing the work. She is a strong, active young woman who believes a sailmaker should sail. She owns a heavy gaff-headed sloop with a topsail in the Caribbean, plans to cross the Atlantic in the spring and cruise in the British Isles in the summer. She has crossed the Atlantic several times and visited harbors up and down the East Coast and in the Caribbean. She gave me great confidence in her knowledge of how a gaff topsail should be cut.

She drove an awl into the floor, measured out the luff of the sail, and drove in another. Then, with two steel tapes, each made fast to one of the awls, she measured out the foot and leach simultaneously, one tape in each hand. Where they came together, she drove in another awl to mark the clew and then measured across the mitre to check that there was no mistake. She snapped a chalk line on luff, leach, and foot and then laid down a strip of cloth from luff to clew.

It is important to get the weave of the cloth going the right way. Ordinary Dacron sailcloth is woven from long fibers of Dacron, made by squirting liquid plastic through small holes like those in a shower head. Oceanus cloth has the same extruded fibers running in one direction but in the other direction a yarn is used spun from short, fine fibers of Dacron like what might be picked out of old rope. The result is a soft, flexible cloth with great resistance to stretch in one direction and good stability in the other and with all the other admirable qualities of Dacron. When wet, it does not soak up water, nor does it mildew. It is light, strong, and resists chafe.

Jinny laid the cloths so the long fibers lay along the mitre, the

ABOVE: **Laying out the first two cloths of the topsail.**
OPPOSITE: **Reinforcing the corner at the tack of the topsail.**

line of greatest strain. She laid down successive cloths, overlapping their edges and marking the overlap so that in sewing them together, she would not pucker the seam by pulling one a little tighter than the other. A topsail is cut quite flat, so the overlaps were about equal across the sail; in a larger sail that needs more draft or fullness, the overlap is less near the luff and greater near the leach.

When I came back in the afternoon, she had sewn the cloths together and was laying out the reinforcements on the corners. Each corner was strengthened by four triangles of sailcloth, two

on each side with their points into the corner and so arranged that the extruded fibers lay along the same lines as those in the sail and so that the seams did not come over each other. She stapled the five thicknesses together to hold them for sewing.

While she sewed them up, I moved over to the end of the loft where Nat was sewing in cringles on the corners of someone else's sail. He sat on a low sailmaker's bench with a rack on one end to hold a fid, spike, and awls, and a tray for needles, twine, and wax. The sail lay across his knees, held with a hook that caught the cloth but did not tear it. Behind him was a picture window framing a view of the Damariscotta River, the Washburn & Doughty Yard, and the C&B Yard. A brigantine lay at the wharf, her yards sent down and her deck covered for the winter.

**Nathaniel S. Wilson, sailmaker**

Several other yachts stored afloat for the winter lay at slips with a few working lobster boats.

Before us lay the cutting floor of varnished hardwood. Windows on three sides gave ample natural light. A big door at floor level on the far end could be opened to lower heavy sails into a truck below. Around the sides were other benches, sewing machines, reels of line, and shelves with thimbles, rings, grommets, snaps, and other hardware. The effect was of quiet orderliness.

While Jinny sewed up the corners of the topsail, and Nat kept on with the cringles, he told me that during the Vietnam War he was in the Coast Guard at New London. Among other unattractive occupations, he was set to painting in a poorly ventilated space and was affected by the fumes. He was transferred to the sail loft, a light, airy place with music. He quickly learned the basic skills of sailmaking while building sails for the Coast Guard bark *Eagle* and was sent to sea with *Eagle's* sails. He taught other Coastguardsmen as they repaired damaged sails and built new ones. When he left the Coast Guard, he worked at Mystic Seaport building sails for smaller vessels and then came to Boothbay to set up his own shop. Although he does most of his work on yachts, many of them quite small yachts—he built a spinnaker a little bigger than a table napkin for our Turnabout—he has built sails for coasting schooners that carry passengers and for school ships described as "tall ships." Most recently, he has built topsails for *Constitution*. He has made a full suit of sails for *Eastward* and individual sails as needed. He is a widely recognized authority on the history, technology, and practical craft of sailmaking.

He told me that the essential aerodynamics of sails were well established by the 1930s and that there have been few changes since except those demanded by changes in sailcloth. A sail should act like an airplane wing on end with the forward part cut full and the after part flat, so that the "lift" acts at right angles to the boom with both a sideways and a forward component. The sideways component is largely neutralized by the reluctance of a sailboat to move sideways through the water, and the forward component is maximized by her eagerness to go ahead. In the days of cotton duck sails, which stretched under strain, this aerodynamic curve was achieved by cutting the foot, luff, and head of the sail in a slightly convex curve. When the sail was laced to a straight spar, the cloth stretched into the right shape.

With the development of stronger and more stable sailcloth, the curve could be cut right into the sail by making the seams between the cloths narrower at the forward end and wider at the after end. Even more stable plastics have recently been developed, about as flexible as sheet iron, leading to increasingly innovative and efficient sails. However, the Oceanus cloth that Nat developed has much of the stability of Dacron and the kindly feel of cotton duck. Nat was my first and only choice for a sailmaker.

All this time, except for a brief visit to Maine Medical Center, I was working in the mornings on a variety of pressing literary projects, including this book, and on the rigging in the afternoons, both with frequent interruptions. One of the most pleasant of these was a visit from my brother Donald with a variety of wooden cleats and a rough ladder, a trial run for the companionway. We repaired at once to *Dorothy Elizabeth*'s cockpit, set the cleats where we thought they might be, discussed their sizes and fastenings. Then we fitted, measured, and marked the ladder and just enjoyed sitting in the cockpit.

November froze and snowed its way into December with the usual Thanksgiving and Christmas crunches. It was all fun, but little progress was made on *Dorothy Elizabeth*. As the solstice passed and the year's candle flickered out, I did a church presentation on the enduring value of an anchor to windward and looked ahead hopefully to a new year afloat.

# XVI

## RATE, TIME, AND DISTANCE

ALMOST AS SOON AS WE KNEW WE WERE GOING TO BUILD *Dorothy Elizabeth*, my sister Ellen claimed the privilege of donating a compass, a compass I was to choose.

The right compass is important. It stands in its binnacle in the center of the cockpit, directly in front of the wheel. Even when not steering by compass, the helmsman is always aware of it and so is everyone else. It represents security in an otherwise fluid and uncertain environment. It keeps us oriented to the Earth's magnetic lines of force, and through these influences we orient ourselves to our Earth's axis, to the North Star, and to the universal geography. When fog erases all the world beyond the next gray wave, a look at the steady compass card tells us we are heading steadily for our next mark, that we are not lost, that we are in tune with terrestrial and cosmic systems. To be more blunt, it tells us where we are going and that the navigator can trust it.

Seal Cove on the Canadian island of Grand Manan is close to one of the busiest fog factories on the East Coast. It had been working overtime all night, and on one particular morning in 1974 in *Eastward* it had exceeded itself. As we left the float, swung around and headed for Southwest Head and the United States, a cheery fisherman called, "Better go back, Cap. It's too thick." I turned to make a response, the boat was still circling, and the wharf faded out. I turned to the compass, but the course was all wrong! If I steered as the compass told me, I knew we would not anywhere near make the mark. Was there a knife in the binnacle? Was there a bucket in the cockpit? No. What to do? I could not even tell the way back. I soon decided that there was a greater chance of my being wrong than there was of the Earth's having changed its magnetic field. I steered the course and we made our mark.

So what kind of a compass should we get? A spherical compass is steadier than a flat-topped one and can be internally gimbaled, that is, the card stays steadily horizontal when the boat pitches or rolls. It should have a jeweled bearing for sensitivity and longevity. And I wanted a card graduated in both points and degrees. I consulted our friend and supplier, Ridge White of Robert E. White, Nautical Instruments, family and commercial descendant of Kelvin and Wilfred O. White who sold nautical instruments a century ago. Ridge told me a card marked in points was not available. They didn't make them anymore. They were obsolete, antiques. Compasses come in degrees only. Everyone can count; almost no one can *box the compass*—name the 32 points in order.

Why, then, seek a card marked in points? First, because it is traditional. Captain John Smith's compass was marked in points in 1614. So was the compass aboard USS *Enterprise* in her battle with HMS *Boxer* off Pemaquid in 1814. The clippers, the Downeasters, the great coal schooners, the Gloucester fishermen, called their courses in points. Irving Johnson, piloting *Yankee* into Newport Harbor at night, called directions aft to me at the wheel. "Starboard a half."

Secondly, there is little likelihood of confusion. North, east, south, and west sound very different from each other, even in a gale of wind. Each quadrant is divided and subdivided, clearly

The shaded diamonds are, clockwise: NNE, ENE, ESE, SSE, SSW, WSW, WNW, NNW. The shaded triangles are "by" points as NxE at 11¼ and SWxS at 213½. "By" points take their names from the nearest cardinal or intercardinal points.

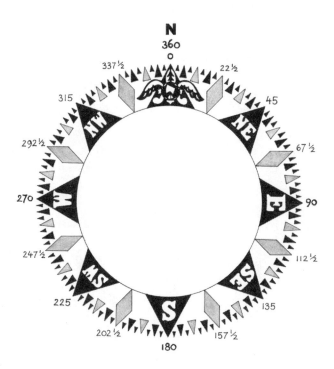

marked on the compass card in a logical pattern and clearly distinguished audibly. One says "nor'west" and "no*th*east" with a hard *th* for the easterly quadrant. Similarly, it is sou'west and sou*th*east. "East-sou*th*east" doesn't sound anything like "south-sou'west," or any other point.

When we were taking boys cruising as an educational exercise—we called it Apprentice Cruises—I set courses in degrees, thinking it would be easier for the boys. When we found ourselves far from our plotted course because the helmsman was steering 166° instead of 156°, I switched to giving courses in points. The boys quickly learned to box the compass and went home quite proud of it.

The implied accuracy of degrees versus quarter points in steering is negligible, for no one can steer a sailing vessel within a quarter point (2.8°) each side of the course; certainly not within a degree. The errors average out.

If someone tells me Seguin Light was bearing 204°, I can't tell where he was without doing some mental arithmetic. Southwest ¾ south tells me at once that that man is in among the wicked ledges northeast of Seguin. I like to remember my course home as east by north, not 079°, and eastward is not the same as 090°. And that is why I want my compass card graduated in points.

Then why fuss with degrees? All calculations in celestial navigation are in degrees. The *Nautical Almanac* gives altitudes and azimuths in degrees. The calculations for correcting compass deviation must be done in degrees. Can you imagine multiplying SE x S ½ S by 2 or subtracting 1¾ points from WNW? The degrees are necessary and convenient for guests who cannot box the compass but can count. With one of these at the wheel, however, the skipper will do well to glance at the compass occasionally from a tactful distance, a distance from which degrees may be indistinguishable but the pattern of the card is clear.

Therefore, I insisted on a card marked in both points and degrees. Ridge could not find one with a 4-inch card but finally found one with a 5-inch card, which I took gratefully. I contemplate building a binnacle suitable to it.

Once installed in its binnacle and lined up parallel to the vessel's keel, it must be corrected, for any large body of ferrous metal—the engine for instance—will give it fits. I will summon a professional compass adjuster who will set up an azimuth instrument on the centerline of the boat and take the sun's bearing with the boat headed north by her own compass. If the sun's bearing is not as calculated, he will note the error and do the same for east, south, and west. Then he will install magnets in the binnacle to compensate for the errors; check the errors, if any, on the intercardinal points; and give me a deviation card listing any residual error. Then I will *know* that my compass points north.

Inadvertent errors are sometimes introduced. One foggy afternoon we took a party out of Newagen. As soon as we lost sight of land, nothing seemed right. The lighthouse with its fog signal was in quite the wrong place. Ledges appeared where no ledges should be. After a short panic, we found a light meter in a camera bag leaning against the binnacle.

The clipper ship *Flying Scud* was struck by lightning, and her cargo of steel rails was magnetized. Her skipper mounted his compass on a plank over the side until his cargo returned to normal. So, given proper attention, a good compass tells you where you are going. You need a clock to tell you how long you have been on the way. It is well, even in these days of quartz watches, to have a clock permanently mounted within view of the chart table and the wheel to keep "ship's time." Thus the navigator always uses the same clock.

When I was in college, my father gave me a ship's clock that struck bells. It was a picturesque addition to the dormitory suite in which three of us lived, but when I left college to teach at a boarding school, I was assigned a very small room. Even with the striking mechanism turned off, the clock's loud tick kept me awake. So I traded that clock at Kelvin White's for a nonstriking clock with a scarcely audible tick. I used it at that school, aboard my father's sloop *Dorothy*, in which we conducted Apprentice Cruises; in *Eastward*; in my school office; and at home. When we gave *Eastward* to Bob, I kept the clock. It still keeps excellent time and tells us how long we have been on the way.

Knowing where we were headed and for how long, we could make a good guess at our position if we knew how fast we had been going. For "ordinary" speeds, 3 to 6 knots in most yachts, one can make a pretty good guess by watching the bubbles go by. Or one can drop a chip overboard near the bow and see how long it takes the boat to sail by it. This calls for a quick hand, a sharp eye, and a stopwatch calibrated in tenths of a second.

A *chip log*, on the other hand, measures the distance run in a given time. The chip is a piece-of-pie shaped board about 6 inches on its radii. A bit of lead on its round side keeps it floating vertically. A line wound on a free-running roller is attached to its three corners with a bridle. The line is marked with a knot every 23′ 9″. The chip is dropped overboard, the watch started, and the knots counted as the line runs over the rail. After exactly 14 seconds, the line is stopped. The number of knots plus the fraction of the distance to the next knot is the speed in knots. This method is cheap, fast, and very accurate.

The electronic knotmeter is quicker and more convenient than the chip log; and, when properly calibrated and kept clean of weeds and barnacles, it is quite accurate. However, I carry a chip log to calibrate my knotmeter, to amuse the curious and to educate the ignorant.

The compass tells us where we are going, the log tells us how fast we are getting there, and the clock tells us how long we have been on the way. Thus we have rate, time, and distance.

Rate x Time = Distance

This is the basis for dead reckoning, or deduced reckoning; it's called dead reckoning because it is usually dead wrong. But navigation is not an exact science, merely the basis for making a correct decision with insufficient evidence.

Of course, says the Modern Man, you don't need all that old-time paraphernalia. A GPS, which you can carry in your shirt pocket, will give you course, speed, distance to the next mark, precise position, and Greenwich Mean Time. The Modern Man is right, I suppose, but even GPS is not infallible. I use compass, clock, and log to keep me in tune with universal harmony and use GPS early and often to support my confidence in the basics.

# XVII

## "How's the Schooner Coming, Cap?"

Through the winter of 1997 to 1998 we made significant progress on *Dorothy Elizabeth*. My brother, Don, made a sturdy companionway ladder, really an admirable piece of engineering and craftsmanship. Now that we could get below easily, he and I installed the handrails on the house. Richard had brought them down the day of the Homecoming, but I had been reluctant to install them. They seemed fragile, and I was afraid if I bent them enough to follow the graceful curve of the side of the house they might break. Ralph said, "If they do, it's just a piece of wood. We'll make another." So my brother and I went at it. I wanted to bolt them down to the top of the house, the bolts to run through the beams. Richard had made the supports to match the spacing of the beams. We tried drilling up through the center of the beam, but all the changing angles confused us. What's "straight up" through a beam curved athwartships and then through the top of the house curved both athwartships and fore-and-aft and then through a rail beveled to fit the top of the house with its athwartships curve? The driller's point of view is restricted by his standing on a slanted cabin floor in a dimly lighted cabin with no view of the outside for orientation. We did it, after a near miss that had to be plugged. Once the first bolt was in, the others could be drilled down from on top. None missed the intended beam, but a few were off dead center a little. The perfection with which Ralph and Richard had worked was marred, and I regretted it. Yet there was now something in our boat, imperfect as it was, that we had done ourselves. Anyway, we now had a solid handhold, and I could go forward with confidence.

We also fastened down cleats for fore-, main-, jib-, and staysail sheets. Frank built travelers for fore-, main-, and staysail sheets but installed them before I got to putting down the thrum mats that our cousin David had brought to me in the hospital. However, my mathematical brother perceived their pattern, took them apart, and reworked them around the travelers.

Dave Coffin, Frank's full time engine doctor, hooked up the engine controls. I had thought to do it myself, as it did not appear to involve any complications. But when I studied the engine, I was soon completely confused. An instrument panel with multi-colored wires, a control to stop the engine, and no easily identified shift and throttle controls had me in the fog. Besides, I was busy with the rigging, which I did understand. So Dave went at it. An instrument panel appeared in the cockpit, and suddenly he needed the hand controls, the levers one actually pushes and pulls. I looked in the catalogues—all expensive chrome-y gadgets with horns sticking out at inconvenient angles to catch in the pockets and jackets of those intent on other things. Then Rich Perry called. He does the joinerwork, woodwork, cabinetwork for Frank. He said he had just taken a set of small bronze controls out of an ancient powerboat and sold them to Mott's Marine Salvage. He thought they would be just the thing for us. I called Mott's but got no answer, so drove right up there. The shop, like most marine salvage shops, was a mixture of "antiques," tourist attractions, and unreconstructed hardware from abandoned or rebuilt boats. Brass steering wheels all polished up, an old wooden lobster trap, buoys, net floats, anchors. . . . Greg Mott, when he saw me come in with a checkbook under my arm, immediately asked what I was looking for.

"Engine controls."

He took me to the back shed where there hung many well-used engine controls, none of which I wanted in my cockpit.

"Rich Perry told me he had just sold you a nice one out of an old powerboat."

"Never heard of Rich Perry. Who's he?"

"Works for Frank Luke."

"Don't know him. Don't remember any such control."

I didn't see anything I liked, so wandered out into the shop to see if he might have anything else I could use. A few wooden blocks too big for our little vessel, more steering wheels, a glass case with a used dory compass all cleaned up in a varnished box, a polished brass sextant, and a neat set of bronze engine controls.

"What about that one? Isn't that a set of engine controls?" He took it out. It was heavy, well machined, and well preserved. A really elegant piece of hardware.

"Where did this come from?"

"A guy brought it in just the other day."

"Rich Perry?"

"Ya. That's the guy."

I bought it for about the same price as the catalogue price for the ones I didn't want. It fits in neatly behind the wheel, easily reached and completely out of the way. Dave soon had it hooked up. Rich came aboard and approved heartily.

These were all interruptions in the wire work, but at last all the wire work was done except for two straps. There are as many splices in the standing rigging of a small schooner as there are in that of a 90-footer. There is less distance between them and the wire is smaller, but there are two main shrouds on each side, one topmast shroud on each side, four foremast shrouds, a forestay, a topmast stay, a springstay, two bowsprit shrouds, an inner bob-stay, and a gaff bridle for each gaff. That is a total of 18 wires,

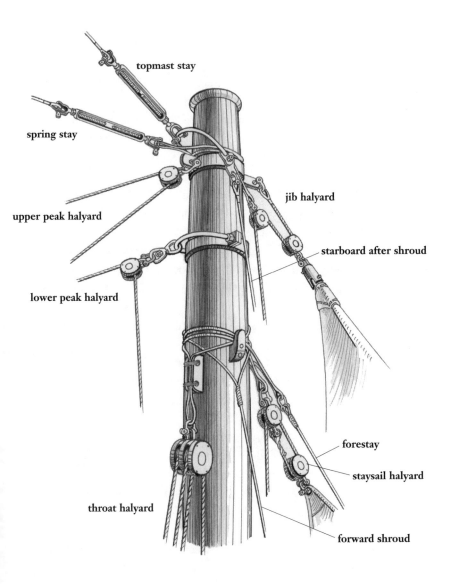

topmast stay

spring stay

jib halyard

upper peak halyard

starboard after shroud

lower peak halyard

forestay

staysail halyard

throat halyard

forward shroud

**Top of the foremast**

each with a splice on each end for a total of 36 splices. That takes an amateur a long time, and it was with no little satisfaction that the last gaff bridle was served up and hung in the garage with all the other coils of wire, each properly labeled. There remained only those two wire straps. A strap is a loop of wire such as might be crudely made by tying together the ends of a 4-foot piece of wire. This, of course, is unacceptable. One was to go around the head of the foremast to take the forward end of the springstay, and the other was to support the upper block of the fore throat halyard.

I had made rope straps and grommets, but I had never made a wire strap. I studied it out in Brion Toss's *Rigger's Apprentice*, but it sounded difficult. Nat said it was no problem. Just unlay a piece of wire a little more than three times the length of the strap. Lay up one of the strands in a loop. . . . He lost me. The idea is to build a new piece of wire by twisting a strand around itself twice, lay in the core, and do it again with another strand, thus building a wire with six strands and a core. I still didn't think I could do it, but I went home and tried. To my surprise and delight, it worked. When the wire was originally laid up, the twist was bent right into it and did not come out when it was unlaid. It was easily laid up again, the twists fitting into each other as easily as Lego blocks. Yet here I was with a loop of wire with four strands and two ends of the core sticking out of it at odd angles. Was it Medusa's head or a crown of thorns? I could see no neat and effective way to finish it off.

Nat slapped the mess into his vise and gave a twist to his marlinespike, and one end of the core disappeared, gone into the wire completely out of sight. So did the other. Then he put a big sail thimble into each end and stretched the strap with a tackle between two posts. With quick, strong fingers, he tied each pair of strands together; pulled, banged, and hammered the knots down into the lay of the wire; tucked each of the two ends;

deftly divided each strand; and tucked it again. And here was a loop of wire with no visible end whatever. All I had to do was take it home and serve it.

Not so easy! It had to be served under tension, so I invented a way to do it. I clamped a pulley for an electric motor in the vise, horizontally, with a dowel down through the shaft hole to keep it steady, the wire lying in the largest groove. A baseball bat lashed to a tackle above and below the wire stretched the loop tight with the diameter, about 2 ½ inches, of the bat, between the parts. I cut off the handle of a serving mallet to fit the spread of the wire and began to serve it up. It didn't go very well because I couldn't turn the mallet and pass the ball of marline between the parts of the wire at the same time. Whenever I dropped the ball, my comments drifted—rocketed—up the stairs. Finally Mary came down and passed the ball, and we finished it up in good shape. The other strap I made myself without Nat's help. Surprisingly easy! I could see what Brion Toss was trying to do with words. I find, myself, that it is much easier to make a strap with wire than it is with words.

That finished the standing rigging. It deserved and received a generous libation that evening.

I painted the upper end of each wire white and tarred the lower ends with a mixture of tar, turpentine, linseed oil, varnish, and drier, and turned back to Cousin Douglas's gaff jaws.

This ought to be easy. Just four jaws and then we hang the rigging on the spars, reeve off the running rigging, step the mates, and launch her.

"Hi Cap. How's the new boat coming on?"

"Great."

"When are you going to launch her?"

"Fourth of July." You have to tell people something.

Now to the gaff jaws. Douglas had left me a pair of jaws an inch thick and an inch wide, curving up to allow for peaking up

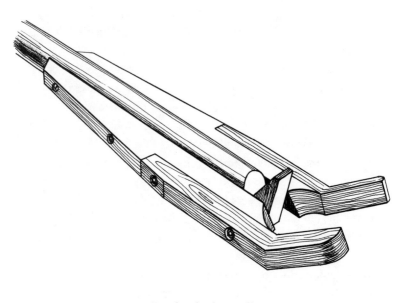

**Jaw for the fore gaff**

the gaff. But the gaff, after I planed it on both sides to provide a flat surface to which to bolt the jaws, was only about 2½ inches wide. The mast around which the jaws must fit was 5½ inches in diameter. Doug had made two wedges to spread the jaws to 6 inches at their tips, but this was still not enough at their inner ends. From a piece of inch-thick oak that Tim Sherman had given me, I cut out spacers to fit and cut them round on the inside to fit around the mast. But it was all wrong. A gaff jaw is not that simple. It has to lie against the mast at an angle of 45° next to the gaff and the pillow block; but at the point where the jaw touches the mast halfway around it, it must lie parallel to the mast. This changing angle must be cut into the block that spaces the Day jaw from the gaff. I could cut one side on the band saw, but the throat of the band saw was too narrow to take the other side. I turned it and twisted it, right side up and upside down—

every way I could think of. I even considered putting on the band saw blade backward, but it wouldn't work. The result of all my efforts was that I spoiled that piece of oak. I had some 1-inch mahogany left over from when we put new garboards in *Eastward* and used that. I wrecked that trying to get the right curves with a saber saw. I also made and wrecked two pillow blocks before I got one that was square to the gaff, perpendicular to the plane of the jaws, and had the right curve to fit the mast. Finally, on June 4, the jaws were done, bolted in place, and covered with leather. The rig for the throat halyard was completed, and on June 7 I took the fore gaff to the yard and set it on *Dorothy Elizabeth*'s deck.

"Hi, Cap. When is the launching?"

"When she's ready, and not a day later."

IT'S THE INTERRUPTIONS that kill you. Maine is Vacationland. The first tour buses crawl around our narrow potholed roads in April. Cars with plates from every state flood in by Memorial Day. Speaking generally, these people come to enjoy the beauties of the coast, the "unspoiled fishing villages," the woods, and the sea. But they have to eat, they need places to sleep, they quickly grow tired of looking at the backs of the necks of other people admiring the simple fishing villages. They seek entertainment. Golf courses, regular and miniature, proliferate. Tour boats take them out to see seals, whales, birds, and offshore islands. Others sail in chartered boats or rent jet skis. Many want to sail their own boats, so boatyards build, store, maintain, and repair scores of yachts. Others sail in party boats, of which *Eastward* is one and *Dorothy Elizabeth* may be another someday. They see souvenirs and "gifts" to take home, browsing (excellent word) through little shops displaying goods made thousands of miles from Maine. There are not enough residents of Maine to take care of all these visitors, so workers from other states throng in too: teachers and college students on vacation wait on tables; gift shop owners and marina workers come from Florida, whence have come many of the vacationers. In short, the town is flooded, inundated, and no one has time even to stoop and tie his shoe.

This hit us too, of course. We had numerous visitors, both family and friends. We were glad to see them, welcomed them enthusiastically, built a fire on the shore and cooked a bucket of lobsters in celebration. But it took time. Weddings, graduations, reunions—they all happen in the summer, and progress on *Dorothy Elizabeth* slows.

One of the most interesting interruptions was rigging our float. Frank had hauled it up in his boatyard in the fall and was ready to hang it on the end of our wharf again. A gangway, a sort of hen walk, extends from the wharf to the float, like a bridge, and serves to keep the float extended from the wharf into deep water. Chains run from the corners of the float to iron rings set in the rock on each side. When Frank came to shackle the chain to one of the rings, he couldn't find it. Mary knew exactly where it was and so did I. We climbed down over the rocks, me with one leg and a cane, went right to the spot, and found no ring. We turned over the wet, heavy weed, even tried cutting out some of it with a knife, but it was too tough and tangled and there was too much of it. I borrowed a metal detector from a real estate agent who used it to find metal boundary markers in the woods, combed over the ledges with that, and no result. Keith Royall, who works for Frank, said he could find it. I stood on the wharf to tell him just where it was. I ought to know. I had hooked up the float every spring for 27 years.

"A little to your left. Now straight ahead. Now one more step ahead. Now, Keith, your right heel is on it." He parted the weed, felt around on the ledge, and *mirabile dictu*, found a hole in the rock with the broken end of the iron down in it.

We remembered that last winter a small red boat with a big

hydraulic mouth on a long steel neck had been slinking along the shore harvesting rockweed, biting off a bushel at a time. We speculated that the creature had eaten up our iron with a mouthful of weed. We got Brad Simmons to bore a new hole and put in a new iron ring.

Back to the jaws. I next tackled the boom jaws. Frank found me a beautiful piece of oak. Boom jaws are all in one plane, have no difficult changing angles, and I had already done one set of jaws. The only interesting difficulty was boring holes for bolts through 8 inches of inch-thick oak and coming out in the middle of the jaw on the other side, neither too high nor too low. I held the electric drill with an extra long bit and lined it up by eye laterally. Mary, sitting in a low chair, squinted along the length of the boom as it lay in the vise with the jaws clamped to it.

"Up a little.

Down a little.

Too much. Up a whisker more."

I pulled the trigger. The motor whirled. Smoke leaked out of the hole, and to our great satisfaction the bit came through the other side pretty much in the middle. We made bolts of ¼-inch bronze rod after we had convinced a clerk in Portland that 5⁄16 rod was not the same as ¼-inch.

On the other gaff jaw, I gave up. I had more twisty oak, but I could not see putting in the time it would take to manufacture another jaw like Doug's. I noticed that the jaws on *Tannis*, a big old rugged Friendship sloop, had no twist upward at all but were extra long so they extended well beyond the mast, even when peaked up. So I did it, salving my conscience with the resolution to make a proper set next winter. The changing angle and the pillow block I had done before. Alec and I took the gaff to the yard on August 12.

Meanwhile, much had been done by others. Frank and his crew had installed a small marine toilet just aft of the foremast.

Donald and I had rigged a foresheet. Bob Ayers of Coastal Marine Electronics had checked out our radio and ordered an antenna, a depth sounder, and a knotmeter for us. Bill Page, formerly of Cannell Payne & Page of Camden, had brought us just the 20-pound Herreshoff anchor we needed and passed a rainy afternoon telling us of buying a fishing boat in Alaska. We were closing in on a launching.

"How's the schooner coming, Cap?"

"Great."

"When's the launching?"

"Labor Day."

# XVIII

## Rigging

WITH THE WIRE WORK AND JAWS DONE, THE ACTION moved to the yard, to the boat itself, and the pace picked up. First we went after the checks in the mast, which Ralph had said should be filled with melted beeswax. I resurrected an alcohol stove set ashore from *Eastward* years ago in favor of a hotter-burning Primus kerosene stove. Cleaned up, and with pump leather renewed and greased, it served to melt the wax in a double boiler. We poured it into the checks from a coffee can with a lip pinched in the rim. It worked, but not very well because the wax congealed before it reached the bottom of the checks. Frank came by, observed our clumsy efforts, and suggested a heat gun to keep the wax liquid. A heat gun is like a super hair dryer, shooting out air hot enough to blister paint. This kept the wax soft enough so we could mush it into the checks with a putty knife. My grandson Roger, Bob's oldest son and a professional photographer, helped with the wax and took pictures.

Now my nephew Curt, his wife, Ruth, and daughter, Anna, turned up from Minnesota and wanted to help. We put them to work at once sanding and painting all the spars. They worked right through lunchtime and finished in time to build a fire on the beach, boil two buckets of lobsters, and put on a family picnic. That was all right. The paint needed time to dry anyway.

As soon as the paint was dry, we brought from the garage those 18 coils of wire rigging and began to hang them on the

Roger S. Duncan

**The skipper pours beeswax in the checks.**

masts. The pace slowed but not the urgency, for we found at once that you can't do anything until you have done everything. We could not put on the shrouds until we had fitted the iron-work. But the irons were a little smaller than the mastheads. So the mastheads must be planed down to fit the irons. But I did not have a bull-nose plane, a plane with the blade in the very front of the sole. I was not going to scour Lincoln County for a bull-nose plane when I had a drawknife hanging in my shop. A drawknife is not a precise and delicate instrument, at least in my hands it isn't, and island spruce has a rough and twisty grain. I got the irons to fit, but the mastheads showed the results of my haste and ineptitude. When I was away, Rich came by, smoothed down the mess I had made, and painted it. Then *that* paint had to dry.

Isn't it remarkable how Rich and Frank and other friends "come by" at opportune times.

Meanwhile, the list of hardware was growing long and longer, hardware we needed before we could step the masts or bend sails. We seized a calm foggy day with Hurricane Bonnie threatening, to visit Bill Page's shop in Cushing. He has gathered a vast collection of new and used yacht hardware, including old-fashioned items not often included in modern catalogues.

Bill is probably the best organized and the most meticulous man in Maine. The boat he built for himself is so finely finished that I would not want to set a glass on the cabin table lest I leave a scratch. His tools are hung neatly over his bench, each with its outline on the wall behind it. Hanging on the side of his table saw and joiner is a push stick with a hole to hang it by. Over the stairs to the second floor is a trapdoor so arranged that heavy things like stoves and anchors can be hoisted conveniently. We found him up there with Brion, a boatbuilder from Brooklin, who was working his way down a shopping list, piling up his purchases on the floor. At first the place looked a little like a supermarket, with rows of shelves holding running lights, blocks, ring bolts, lamps. . . . While Bill was welcoming us, Brion was poking into one of the boxes. Bill stopped that. This was no supermarket. Brion asked for what he wanted and Bill found it, or something like it, or something as good or better, and Brion chose. When the list was complete, Bill and Brion got down on their knees and added up the prices, which were obviously subject to change without notice.

Meanwhile, just below the windows a ketch was moving slowly

to and fro in the St. George River and blowing a horn. Bill ostensibly paid no attention. Presently the horn stopped and shortly after, a woman appeared at the head of the stairs asking if Bill had a mooring for her in Pleasant Point Gut. The Gut is a small, bottle-tight little harbor in which Bill maintains a mooring usually occupied by his own boat. She said the harbor was crowded and they were looking for a place to ride out Hurricane Bonnie. Bill offered a mooring in front of the shop, but that, all right on a quiet night, was wide open to the southeast and no place to be in a hurricane. Bill suggested Vinalhaven 20 miles to the east and asked me, as author of the *Guide*, for my suggestions. She didn't like either Bill's or my suggestions. She obviously wanted a mooring in the Gut but finally suggested Thomaston, about 5 miles up the river. We agreed that Thomaston would be good if she could find room there, and she left. The yacht floated around awhile and at length departed. Bill, adding up Brion's bill, observed that anyone who blew a horn outside his shop expecting him to come running down the shore did not have money enough to buy anything he had. Prices subject to change without notice.

Brion departed and Bill came to us.

"What do you need, Cap?"

"Three cheek blocks."

"Now, what in the world do you need three cheek blocks for?"

"Reef pennants on fore and main booms and one for the topsail sheet." Bill brought out a box from a back shelf. We looked over cheek blocks of different sizes, found two that matched and one that would do very well for a topsail sheet.

"What's next?"

"Navigation lights."

"Running lights! Navigation lights (with great scorn). The man wants *running lights*." Out came a box of new and used running lights, lightweight and very expensive. Of the used ones, some were painted, some not. Some lacked sockets or colored glass. We picked out what we needed, Bill cannibalizing a socket from one, a bulb from another, and a glass here and there.

"Handles to mount flush on the engine hatch." Bill found some new cast brass ones and some old heavy bronze ones, the new ones less expensive. We took the old ones.

Finally, after having piled up quite an order, I asked for a 25-pound CQR plow anchor. Bill exploded all over me.

"What does a fishing schooner want with a plow? A plow is designed to go easily through the soil, and you want it to hold your boat? A fisherman's anchor is the only kind to have." I insisted on a plow and he puttered around and found several smaller ones, but I wanted a 25-pound plow anchor. I could see one lying on the floor next to a Shipmate stove. Finally he stumbled on it.

"Well, you can have this one. It was used just once by a little old lady." We took it.

It is sometimes hard to tell when Bill is kidding. He gave us a very good price on the anchor and, indeed, on everything else, and helped us lug it all to the car. It was raining, so we gave him a lift home and drove back to East Boothbay through late-August thunderstorms.

The summer was fading fast. Students, teachers, and their families were leaving for schools and colleges. Some restaurants and gift shops were closing up. A few yachts coming in for winter storage already lay on Frank's moorings. Cruising boats headed westward. Bob and Alec laid up *Eastward* and they too went back to school and college. It was borne in upon us that if we didn't get *Dorothy Elizabeth* overboard very soon, we would not sail her until next spring. We must press on. We could not afford to lose a day.

We had always been able to rig *Eastward* in two days, but we found that a schooner with two masts takes a lot longer than rigging a sloop with one. Furthermore, on a new boat there are little things and little things and more little things to be done and they take time, time, time. For instance, the fore lower shrouds are spliced around the mast, one on each side. The splices are all made. Just slide the loops over the mastheads and slip them down to where they belong—but first take off the iron on the masthead, which is too big to let the splices go over it. Then, what is to keep the splices at the designed level? We need two oak ears screwed to the mast, one on each side to hold the shrouds and—oh, yes—and the forestay and the strap supporting the fore throat halyard. It should be no trouble to cut out two ears on the band saw. It wasn't; and I made them big enough to support all they had to support. Now, however, the ears were flat and the mast was round. Either the mast must be flattened or the ears given a concave curve to fit around the mast. We don't want to weaken the mast, which seems pretty small already, so how to hollow the inside of the ear? I don't have a hollowing plane. A sanding drum should do it. Even with the ear held firmly in the vise, it is difficult to hold the drum exactly in the middle of the ear, and the drum is smaller than the mast anyway. I tried it and spoiled one ear and had to make another. Cutting the curve with the band saw didn't work because the radius of the curve is so small that it cramps the blade. I solved the problem by wrapping a piece of very rough sandpaper, 36-grit, around the mast and scrubbing the ear up and down on it, bearing down hard. It took about 500 strokes and several pieces of paper, but it worked, at least well enough so bedding compound could make up the difference. There goes a day's work anyway and still the fore lower shrouds are not in place.

A day's work did I say? Only a day's work? With three therapies, a leg and a half, and all the little interruptions the flesh is heir to? That particular problem did not afflict us on the mainmast, but there were others. There was no provision for the two peak halyard blocks. Frank quickly welded an eye on the iron at the head of the lower mast. The proper arrangement for the lower peak halyard block would be a steel band around the mast with a traveler on it for the block. There wasn't time to have that fabricated and fitted, so I fashioned a grommet of ½-inch rope, slipped it over the masthead, and held it in place with two chocks. Quick and dirty perhaps, but next winter we will get a proper band made.

And so it went. We were gaining, but not fast enough to catch Labor Day.

But at my back I always hear
Time's winged chariot hurrying near; . . .

# XIX

## LAUNCHING

LABOR DAY, SEPTEMBER 7, CAME AND WENT. THE NEXT day I told Frank that, if it suited him, we would launch *Dorothy Elizabeth* on Saturday, September 19, the day when the highest tide of the month came at 11:03 A.M. I wrote a news story for the paper and told all our friends. We were committed and we rushed ahead.

But there is always something. Our smoke alarm went off at 3 A.M. Mary, in a rush to get out of bed, fell, hit her head, broke her arm, and wrenched her shoulder. That was a serious setback, but with my brother to help, we pushed on. There was only the running rigging left to do, and that, we thought, should be easy. Mary and I had taken a quick trip to Hamilton Marine in Searsport for life preservers, other Coast Guard–required equipment, 1,200 feet of ⅜-inch Dacron line, 300 feet of ¾-inch nylon for anchor line, and a few items of hardware that Bill Page could not supply.

The next day I took time to build a rack for the coils of Dacron rope so it would come off the reel without kinking. Then Donald and I spliced in and hung on the mast the jib and fore peak halyards. Here is progress! But in drilling out a burr in a hole on the top of the foremast, the drill jammed. It wrecked the chuck. My efforts to fix it made it worse. I swept off the bench the bits and pieces of the drill and the chuck and left them at the dump with a note, "If you can fix it, you can have it," and bought a new drill.

A day later I got Jon Marsh, sign painter, former student of mine, to paint her name on the stern and both bows of *Dorothy Elizabeth*. He did an admirable job, freehand. Now at last she knew who she was.

As we got to hanging upper halyard blocks, we found that all the holes in the irons were 5/16, not 3/8 as I had expected. I bought out the hardware store's stock of 5/16 shackles and never asked the price. You do what you have to do and press on.

Back in the fall of 1996, when *Dorothy Elizabeth* was no more than a gleam in our eyes and Ralph's, I had bought some blocks from Frank, ones that his father had stashed away years ago when

**Launching**

he was building wooden yachts. They were beautifully finished ash blocks with bronze roller bearings but lacking pins and straps. I took them to John to have straps made but told him that of course there was no hurry. He was busy building a tender for South African oil rigs and had passed them to a friend who works in stainless steel. Now, a week before launching, the time had come to hurry and the blocks had been stolen. We could not launch the boat until the upper blocks were in place.

Yacht suppliers do not sell wooden blocks. I called Bill Page. He had none. I called A. Dauphinée in Lunenburg. Yes, he had single blocks and could supply them with beckets as needed. He could ship them the next day.

I still needed two double blocks for main and fore throat halyards. Sometimes the world turns our way. In the mail came two double blocks. Travis Woolcott, who had been my secretary at Belmont Hill, and her husband, John, had spent a night on our mooring in their modern ketch *Another Adventure*. They could not use these antiques in their state-of-the-art plastic and stainless steel yacht. Press on. Press on.

With the spars still laid on horses, Donald and I ran the topmast down through the ring in the upper iron at the head of the mainmast and stepped it in the step made for it in the lower iron. This was difficult because the irons slipped around the mast; the topmast would stand canted either to port or starboard. I took the lower one home to drill a hole for a screw to hold it in place and found my cherished wife, with a broken arm, frying doughnuts for the launching party. It wasn't a bad break, the doctor said. Only a fracture. They were excellent doughnuts. I checked. We got the topmast stepped that afternoon.

With five days and counting to launching day, we were working steadily on the running rigging, rolling Dacron line off the reel at an extravagant rate, splicing it into the beckets on the new Lunenburg blocks, sewing servings on the other ends, shackling the upper ends to the masts. We were slowed occasionally by the necessity to work a grommet, make a chock to hold it on, or find a screw, bolt, thimble, or shackle. Mary, arm and shoulder notwithstanding, moused shackles, spread cotter pins, pushed on with the job. Bob Ayers installed a fuse panel, depth sounder, and knotmeter. Frank, Rich, and the yard crew were busy hauling boats for winter storage but did whatever they could to help us along.

Several times we got unbelievably lucky. We needed six bronze sway hooks. A *sway hook* is a smoothly finished hook with a long threaded shaft to go down through the deck and the shelf and be held with a nut and washer under the shelf. A halyard is led under the sway hook and up to the belaying pin in the pinrail. Its purpose is to take the strain of the halyard and to provide a downward strain on the pinrail. When the halyard is nearly chockablock, one passes the line under the sway hook; grasps the halyard with one hand, holding a turn on the pin with the other; and sways back and down on the halyard, taking up the slack under the hook and on the pin. Sway hooks were common fittings on old-timers but are almost never used today, replaced instead by winches. Standing in his machine shop, I asked Frank if by any odd chance his father would have had a pattern for a sway hook left from the time when he built schooner yachts. Frank didn't know, said maybe there might be but he doubted it. Under the bench was a wide, deep drawer full of hardware. It was very heavy and obviously not in daily use. Frank braced a foot and heaved it open about 5 inches, just enough to get his hand in. He reached around inside and miraculously—no other word describes it—brought out a beautifully polished bronze sway hook of just the right size for *Dorothy Elizabeth*. He heaved the drawer farther open but could find no more and nothing else of the slightest use. With this for a pattern, he could get five more made, get a dozen. They look good at a boat show, he said.

**Swayhook in action**

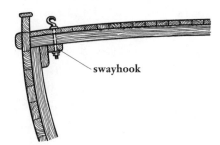

swayhook

Someone will find a use for them.

Three days to launch and counting. Frank called at lunchtime.

"I've got a bunch of guys sitting on their ass waiting and doing nothing. I want to step those masts." We rushed over. *Dorothy Elizabeth* was out of the shed and under the derrick. The spars lay on horses alongside, the rigging all there but more or less tangled up. We took some time straightening it all out, being sure that what was to lead forward was forward of the spreaders. One year on *Eastward* I had the topmast stay, which goes to the end of the bowsprit, leading aft. That took some fixing.

Bob Ayers brought the radio antenna and lead wire, which we screwed to the spreaders and taped to a topmast shroud. Then Mary climbed the ladder to *Dorothy Elizabeth*'s deck and disappeared below to put in each mast step a real silver Canadian dime given by our New Brunswick sailing friend, Gerry Peer, who had helped us substantially with the *Guide*. He instructed us to put the coin *Bluenose* up and sailing forward. In ancient days, a launching was celebrated with sacrifices to the gods. Norse boatbuilders sent slaves under a boat to be launched, to knock out the blocks on which she was resting. They often became human sacrifices. In the nineteenth century it was customary to put a gold coin under a mast step, "for luck." You can't get a gold coin now, so a real silver one will have to do. Mary also included a real copper Lincoln penny. Rich brought us a neat little bronze block for a main flag halyard. Keith and Frank rigged a sling on the foremast and, suddenly, there it was up in the air, everything dangling. It hung for a moment, poised over the vessel, and eased down into its step.

As we were about to lift the mainmast, it was evident that the lower iron had turned in spite of the screw we had put in it. We got the screw out. Rich bored two more holes in the iron and put in two big screws. Up went the mainmast and clunked into its step, the rigging hanging every whichway because we had had to turn the mast over several times to get that ring straight and firmly fastened.

Keith swarmed up the derrick boom, a girder about a foot wide, untangled the rigging above the spreaders, and shackled the springstay and the topmast stay to the top of the foremast. The yard crew had already worked overtime and left, leaving Donald, Mary, and me to straighten things out. We bolted the lower deadeyes to chainplates and rove off lanyards hand tight— at least enough to keep the spars more or less vertical—rigged the forestay, and called it a day.

I went down on the shore with the sun setting behind me to see how she looked. In that clear, golden light she was the most beautiful thing I had almost ever seen—that I had ever seen. The spars brought her grace, made what had been an admirable boat no longer merely a collection of bolts and shackles, wire and wood, but a single, integrated work of art, the visible expression of our original wisdom.

Two days and counting.

Early that morning, before we started the day, it occurred to me that the springstay was too long and the topmast stay too short. To make adjustments, someone would have to go up the foremast sometime. With no sway hooks and no pinrails, it would be more than difficult. It would be much quicker and easier to have Keith go up the derrick boom while the boat was still under it.

So I was at the yard by seven o'clock. Frank had the tractor hooked to the trailer on which the boat sat, ready to move her out of the way of the railway. But with his unusual accommodating and flexible good nature, he mentally readjusted his schedule and sent Keith up to do the job. He had to add 10 inches of chain to the topmast stay and substitute a smaller turnbuckle for the one I had on the springstay. I will make new stays next winter. Home to breakfast.

Donald set up the rigging, greasing the deadeyes with kitchen grease and setting up the lanyards with the tackle we were to use for the jackstay.

Perhaps in a computerized boatyard producing a single model of a fiberglass boat, sudden prelaunch crises are unknown. Frank Luke tells me, however, that in most yards, even the best managed ones like his, there are always unexpected emergencies. Every compromise made in the whole course of planning and construction must be paid for before the champagne bottle is broken. And so it was with us.

All day long we ran into one thing after another. The fore boom was too long to swing clear of the mainmast. I found the bag with the foresail, spread out the sail, measured its foot, and found we could take 6 inches off the boom and still leave enough to stretch the sail.

Then to finishing the pinrails for the fore-, main-, and stay-sail halyards. They must be drilled at the proper angles to fit the shrouds and the belaying pins, at angles that would look right. With three pinrails to mark, take home, and drill, this kept me busy for quite a while. Donald was untangling halyards and topping lifts and sheets, making their lower ends fast to gaffs and deck with shackles, splices, or cotter pins.

We put 1,500 pounds of lead between the floor timbers in the bilge. The lead came in 5-pound cakes joined together in groups of four, which would just fit between the floor timbers.

Somewhere in here Thursday became Friday, with the usual intervals of eating and sleeping, but my journal does not mark the transition.

The roll-up jib lay in the car, coiled like a huge anaconda. I had never rigged one before and hardly knew where to start. Nat had included the reel and swivel for the tack. With the help of a ladder rather shakily leaning against the bowsprit, I attached the reel to the bowsprit. Frank found a swivel for the head of the sail, perhaps in that magic drawer whence came the sway hook. I hoisted the jib, still rolled up, and it hung discouragingly limp. Nat had specified that the halyard should be fast at the top of the foremast, leading to a block at the head of the sail, thence to a block lower down on the foremast, thence to the deck. This rig would prevent the halyard from twisting as the sail rolled or unrolled. Yet when hoisted, the block on the head of the sail came only to the lower block on the mast. Donald and I, craning our necks until we were stiff, thought of several ways to solve the problem, none easily and none without going up there. The yard crew had gone home for the day and the sun was already in the trees across the bay. We gave up and started for home.

But it occurred to us as we were leaving that the launching was the next morning and we should have the United States ensign at the taffrail and the burgee of the Cruising Club of America at the head of the foremast. Four screws and a fitting already on hand solved the ensign problem. I could borrow *Eastward*'s staff and flag in the morning. We had a flag halyard rigged on the foremast and a staff to carry the burgee above the top of the mast. We bent on the burgee, and Don took a photograph of me hoisting it. We started for home again.

But we had not reached the ladder before one end of the halyard dropped down on deck and the staff bent limply over. The end of the halyard holding the bottom end of the stick had let go, and the weight of the line from the block to the deck was greater than the weight of the burgee and the staff, so we could not get it down. We rigged a bosun's chair on the staysail halyard, and I tried to hoist Don, holding a turn on the staysail traveler for lack of a pinrail and sway hook. Don weighs more than I do, but even with the advantage of the tackle and with Don pulling on the halyard as much as he could, we could not get him high enough. Fortunately, there was a long boathook lying in the scuppers, and with that Don hooked the stick and got it down. The halyard had been tied to a screw eye in the end grain at the bottom of the stick and it had pulled out. We clove-hitched the halyard to the stick, tried again without a photograph, and departed in the dusk.

Why must we make our own gaff jaws and fit chocks to our spars? Ralph and Richard could do it faster and better. Why must we do our own rigging, pour beeswax, and mouse shackles?

The first saltwater people I ever knew, except my father, were New Harbor fishermen—self-sufficient, independent people. Captain Ed McFarland built several of his own lobster boats. I watched him build his last one. Captain Riley McFarland, with whom I went lobstering, built his own traps, mended his own nets, maintained his own wharf and lobster car, built his own punt. Only summer people hired help.

We admired these fishermen and their community. Under their eyes we learned to row, sail, scull a punt, and set a trawl. Captain Ed said, "Knowledge earned is better than knowledge learned if it don't come too dear." He let us alone to earn what we could and saved us from paying too dear. We were proud of our growing independence.

Just out of my teens, I met Hal Vaughan, a man of explosive energy and ingenuity. Among other things, he ran a sailing camp for boys on Birch Island in Penobscot Bay. He rigged a generator to his kerosene pump engine, filled his overhead water tank after dark, and so had water all day and electricity in the evening. When he wanted to haul a boat up the beach, he coupled two Chevrolet transmissions in tandem to a Chevrolet engine, built a winch from a differential gear and a spruce log. He slapped both transmissions into low gear and twitched the boat in her cradle up the beach on rollers.

Mary's father had her threading pipe, tearing out a partition, carpentering, and setting glass in their colonial house. We finished out, rigged, and maintained our sloop *Eastward*, set out our own moorings, hauled our own float.

Of course we needed help, for we had neither the time, the skill, nor the equipment to make proper sails, to step masts, or to drive piles for wharves. We sought help when we needed it and found skillful people always eager to share their skills with those who wanted to learn.

The most important reason for doing as much of our own work as we did was that everything we ourselves put into *Dorothy Elizabeth* made her that much more our boat. Had we told Ralph to go ahead and build her, just let us know when she was ready to sail away, she would have been his boat, not ours. Now she is ours and Ralph's and Frank's and Nat's. All of us who built her are part of her, from Andy cutting bungs to Jon Marsh painting her name on her stern. That's the kind of boat we are proud to sail.

WE HAD LEFT THE JIB in its rolled-up mode, hanging limply. It came to me, again early in the morning, on launching day that the solution was to ask Nat. He had built the sail. So I called him as early in the morning as was decent, and he came down to the yard at once. He tucked a splice in each end of a short piece of line, and we waited for Frank. The tide was coming fast.

Frank, unperturbed, said, "Let's play boatyard." He moved the boat, already on the trailer, under the derrick. He asked Nat if he were used to derricks. Nat, who had worked aloft on *Eagle* and many yachts, answered that he was getting that way and up he went. He passed the line twice around the top of the foremast, with the splices hanging down on either side of the halyard, then shackled the splices into the block. When hoisted, the jib was not as tight as we would have liked but was much better than it had been. When swayed up as tightly as we could get it, the halyard was not yet chockablock.

Frank moved the boat on to the railway. The tide was coming.

Meanwhile grandsons Alec and Mark had set up planks on horses, and Mary and Joyce laid down a cloth weighted with

Coke cans. The chilly southwest breeze blew away the cloth. Frank, up to any emergency, found 5-pound lead muffins to hold it down.

Mary, who had made almost all preparations herself in spite of sore shoulder and arm, with help from Joyce, Nora, and Verna, laid out doughnuts, lemon cake, crackers and cheese, and cookies. There was a tub of ice with cans of soft drinks and beer, and a big urn of coffee was brewing. Donald rigged a new staff for the burgee, and the ensign flew bravely over the taffail. Peggy Miner, Frank's sister, prepared a champagne bottle, first with tape to contain flying glass and then with blue ribbons. She instructed Mary on christening techniques.

People drifted in. We had announced the event in the paper and spread the word to everyone we knew in post office, store, YMCA, and church. We had specially invited those who had worked on the boat, including Ralph, Marion, Richard, and the Butlers from Mount Desert. Bill Tefft was there to record the event on film. Our sons Bob and Bill and grandsons Alec and Mark had made long journeys to get there. There must have been 100 people gathered for the Event.

The tide crept up and the clock crept close to 11. Frank had everything ready: the trailer chained to the platform, the hoisting gear clear, Keith on the wharf with a line. Dave Coffin climbed aboard to run the engine. Bob came aboard to handle lines, and I came aboard last. Frank took away the ladder. Peggy helped balance Mary on a plank under the bow, the focus of 50 cameras. Frank said his father always launched on a rising tide. The tide was to be high at 11:03. At precisely eleven o'clock, Mary whacked the bottle on the bobstay fitting. It didn't break. She stepped back, swung with her good arm. In a shower of foaming champagne, Frank started the railway down. Donald, arrayed in full Highland regalia, Cameron kilt, sporran, and bonnet, skirled the pipes. The water of Linekin Bay came up under

Barbara Freeman

*Dorothy Elizabeth*. She caught her balance, floated off the trailer. She was launched.

The rest was celebration. Dave started the engine, backed off against the wind, swung around into a slip. She steered just as any good boat under power would steer, behaved herself like a lady.

People came aboard and admired. Donald continued on the pipes with his best tunes, particularly "Fair Harvard" and "Scotland the Brave." People congratulated us, clustered around the table, demolished the good things Mary had prepared, rejoiced that at last we had done it.

Afloat, *Dorothy Elizabeth* looked much smaller against the background of a big ocean, but neat, trim, and tucked up if a bit down by the stern to a critical eye.

*Dorothy Elizabeth* and Donald C. Duncan

# XX

## UNDER WAY

AFTER LUNCH, BEARING THE FORESAIL, AN ANCHOR, AND line, Mark, Alec, and I found *Dorothy Elizabeth* lying in the slip where we had left her, looking quite used to being afloat. We bent on the sail, stretching head and foot tightly, lashing mast hoops as we had on *Eastward*, impressed by how small and light was all the gear compared to *Eastward*'s mainsail.

We made the bitter end of the anchor line fast to the bitt below the deck, coiled the rest of the line carefully down the fore hatch, and laid the anchor on the coil. Having once got under way alone in the old *Dorothy* without this ritual, I found myself anchoring in a hurry on a lee shore with a rat's nest of anchor line that wouldn't even come up the fore hatch. I shook out enough scope to save the ship, but such ritual has its purpose.

Mary and Bob showed up, we started the engine, backed out of the slip, headed into the wind. The boys set the foresail. I stopped the clattering engine and in the silence, bore off. The sail slatted once and filled. *Dorothy Elizabeth* heeled a bit to the southwest breeze and sailed, sailed a little tentatively, but sailed.

It was probably as much I who was tentative as *Dorothy Elizabeth*. I had no idea how this new boat would react to sail and wind and sea. She was like all the other small boats I had sailed, yet she was not the same as any. She could be a great disappointment, and I so wanted her to be a delight. I was looking for her good qualities and I found them. She slipped through the water easily, just as we thought she would when we first looked inside her after she was planked. Even under foresail alone, there was a ripple at her bow and scarcely an eddy under her stern. She responded well to the wheel, although under such short sail she lacked power.

I was prepared to be disappointed too. Even with the foresail sheeted as flat as we could sheet it, she would not sail closer than about 6½ points (70°) to the wind. The fore traveler was too long. Perhaps the sail was cut too full or perhaps we had not set it properly. Maybe it needed a tack downhaul. I tried several times to tack her, but under such short sail she could not build enough momentum to get through the eye of the wind—maybe because we were towing the dory. I made excuses for her.

We reached out across the bay, making a little better than a "square drift," and each of us had a short trick at the wheel. We were to windward of our mooring so jibed, and with the sheet eased, headed home. She picked up speed. The bubbles slipped easily by the lee side and merged with the little eddies of the wake. Still no ugly quarter wave astern.

We approached our familiar mooring fast enough to luff alongside it, and Alec's long arm did the work of a boathook. We rowed ashore. Mark tied up the dory, and I followed my crew up the gangway. I stopped on the wharf and looked back. There she lay, our little schooner, very easy to look at, on her own mooring at last. I had sailed her up to it, skipper on our own boat again after two years ashore. I had made the decisions. I was responsible for her. She was ours. I stumped up the hill after the others.

That night our sons took us all out to dinner to celebrate the occasion. We raised a glass to my mother, Dorothy, and to half the people who had put *Dorothy Elizabeth* on the mooring where she now lay. Then we raised another glass to Mary's mother, Elizabeth, and to the other half of the people who had put her on that mooring. You can't row with one oar.

Still, *Dorothy Elizabeth* was not ready to go to sea. We were blessed with cool, pleasant September weather to do what remained. My brother Don came over every afternoon. We brought the schooner alongside our float, handy to our shop, and the three of us, Mary, Don, and I, went at it.

Before you can do anything, you have to do everything. For example, take one sail, the roll-up jib. We could not hoist it, or any other sail, without sway hooks. We motored back to the yard to have Rich install them and, incidentally, to ease the fore hatch, which stuck when wet. That took one day and part of another. We could not set the jib, although it was hoisted like a great sausage to the foremast head, until the sheets were rove off. But we had to set it to determine where on the deck the eyebolts and fairleads should be put. And we could not unroll it until Nat could come down and swage an eye in the end of the wire that rolls up in the drum. We couldn't call Nat until we had screwed a fairlead to the bowsprit so that same wire running through it would wind properly on the drum. When we had the wire running through the fairlead and the eye swaged to it, we spliced a light line to the eye and led it aft to the cockpit coaming. But we had to screw a cleat to the coaming to which to belay that line. Donald had made the cleat the winter before. Now we could unroll the jib and figure where on the deck to put the eyebolts and fairleads. They should lead the sheet about 5° below the line of the mitre. I spent a long and very uncomfortable afternoon coiled under the foredeck with the anchor digging into my back, putting washers and nuts on the U-bolts holding the fairleads to the deck above.

With an eyebolt and a fairlead on each side, are we at last ready to reeve off the sheets? No. We need a bridle on the clew of the sail with a bullet block on each end, bullet blocks from Bill Page's loft. At last! Up to the garage for line for the two sheets, splice into the eyebolts, lead it through the bullet blocks, back to the fairleads, and aft to the cleat, installed last winter. Sew a whipping on the loose ends. Now cast off the line to the drum, pull on a sheet. The sail unrolls with a snap, fills without a wrinkle. Glorious to behold. Pull on the roll-up line. The sail disappears. And this has taken several days.

We did much the same sort of thing with the staysail. Mary and I spent a foggy soggy afternoon on the mainsail, and as the early October dusk gathered in we hoisted it at last. By the time we had admired it sufficiently, lowered it, furled it, put the vessel back on her mooring under power, and rowed ashore, it was black dark, but she was ready to sail under four lowers.

Somewhere in here I had moved 250 pounds of lead forward from the after bay to the bay ahead of the foremast to trim her better.

The next afternoon, Donald and I fiddled, filed, and fitted with the topsail, but darkness fell that day before we finished.

On Sunday, October 4, two weeks after launching, Mary and I, moving slowly with three legs and three arms between us, got under way under mainsail, foresail, staysail, and jib and struck out across the bay. It was a cool Indian summer day with a moderate southerly breeze. *Dorothy Elizabeth* leaned to it, almost to her rail, and slipped through the water like a mackerel. There was little turbulence in the wake and still no quarter wave. We were just getting the feel of her when a late-blooming powerboat came by, recognized this as our first sail, circled us slowly, waving congratulations and taking pictures. We beat down the bay, finding that she didn't point high but sailed very well, and she felt like a bigger vessel than she was.

Out in Boothbay Harbor we were hailed by Captain Herb Smith in the big schooner *Appledore*. He sailed around us to give his passengers a treat and welcomed us to the Boothbay Harbor fleet. Then Captain Bob Campbell in the Squirrel Island ferry, *Novelty*, saluted us enthusiastically. Welcomed and applauded by such distinguished seamen, we ran home before the wind, wing and wing, sinfully proud.

The following day a cold front blew the summer away with a strong northwest breeze. Our son John and his wife, Carol, were visiting from North Carolina, so there could be no thought of staying ashore. With Donald and Joyce to help, we reefed the mainsail and sailed under mainsail, foresail, and staysail. She buried her rail in the puffs, but once her rail was in the water, she seemed quite stiff. She balanced well, sailed quite fast on the wind, and ran like smoke before the wind.

Two days later we finally tamed the topsail but found that the whole rig needed tightening up and tuning. A lady's wardrobe needs proper adjusting for her to look her best.

Now the Indian summer weather caved in. We had agreed last spring to participate in the 75th anniversary celebration of the Belmont Hill School where I had taught for 31 years, so we left *Dorothy Elizabeth* on one of Frank's heavy moorings and headed for Massachusetts in the rain.

It rained for three days and three nights—hard. The weather bureau reported 9 inches in three days. It was still raining when we got home about four o'clock in the afternoon. Remembering that any water falling into *Dorothy Elizabeth*'s big cockpit would find its way inevitably into the bilge, it seemed wise to row up to Frank's and see how she was making it. We donned oilclothes, bailed out the dory, which was almost awash, and found *Dorothy Elizabeth* looking very uncomfortable indeed, her red waterline almost submerged and her motion awkward and logy in the choppy water. Aboard, I found the water in the cabin up to the bilge clamp amidships, about 18 inches over the floor. The floorboards and everything else that would float was floating, the red watertight box of flares bobbing cheerily about over all. But the radio and the tool box couldn't swim. I applied myself at once to that master of a bilge pump, very glad for a handle that came waist-high and worked fore and aft and not up and down. That pump really moved water, but the day was pretty well used up and so was I when at last I heard it suck air. I didn't go below. It was wet, dark, and cold. What was wet couldn't get any wetter and certainly would not dry out. So leave it. As we rowed home in the dark and rain, I thought favorably of an automatic electric bilge pump and was very grateful for the pump we had.

The next day I cleaned things up. When one picks up a wet cardboard box, one finds oneself holding a soggy mess of cardboard in both hands and contemplating what had been the contents of that box in a heap at one's feet. YUK! However, tools were cleaned and oiled, the radio dried out, checked by Bob Ayers and found to be healthy and the batteries undamaged. The flood had reached no vital part of the engine.

We soon found a chance to tame the topsail, set up rigging, and improve performance. But the summer was over. The winds were heavier and colder, the afternoons shorter with only a skim milk sun.

We wanted to get Nat to come out with us and critique our rig and the way our sails were set, but a succession of days too windy for the purpose put that off. We did get a few chances to sail between gales.

On October 17 we arranged with Frank to take Bill Tefft, the *WoodenBoat* photographer, in his powerboat to take pictures of *Dorothy Elizabeth* under sail. Ralph and Marion Stanley joined us from Southwest Harbor, and Bob from Concord. With a light southwest breeze and under full sail, *Dorothy Elizabeth* looked her best. Donald in his sloop *Heather* escorted us and also took pictures. Bill transferred aboard us after he had done all he could from Frank's boat, and we had a pleasant sail, gaining confidence in what she could do and knowledge about what she couldn't. Ralph seemed really pleased about what we had built.

The climactic experience came the next day. We invited our

Bill Tefft

old friend, ally, and shipmate Hugh Williams to join us, and Bob was still with us. With these two experienced seamen to help, we got the sails to set better than ever. We sailed closer to the wind as we beat out of the bay. Out where we could see a wide stretch of sea horizon, we found a rail breeze and for the first time, a bit of a sea running. She loved it. We loved it. She lifted her bow to a crest, bore down hard into the trough, filled the lee scuppers, wet the lower deadeyes, and drove ahead at the next sea. No pounding, no hesitation, no feeling of being overdriven, no hard-boiling wake or ugly stern wave.

OPPOSITE: **Ralph and Marion Stanley.** ABOVE: **Skipper at the wheel.**

You can't go to windward forever. We bore off around the end of Fisherman Island in the same rut *Eastward* had worn in the water for many years between the Hypocrites Ledge and another unnamed. On a broad reach, she tucked up her skirts and hustled, like a lady running for a bus. The knotmeter read 7.5. The wake was boiling, and now there surely was a wave under the stern. Yet she balanced well and steered easily.

In the narrow part between the ledges, we had to swing her stern through the eye of the wind, to tack or jibe. I elected to tack. Accordingly, I turned hard toward the wind and trimmed the mainsheet to help her around. Bob and Hugh eased jib, staysail, and foresail sheets. She rounded into the wind, and as she fell off on the other tack, the crew trimmed headsail sheets and I started to slack the mainsheet. But the mainsheet had taken itself a turn or two around the wheel spokes and my game leg. I could neither turn the wheel nor slack the sheet. Under full sail with a fresh breeze, *Dorothy Elizabeth* was sailing fast directly toward the ledge perhaps 150 yards ahead. I didn't look. I was very busy trying desperately to clear the mainsheet. The crew, at first unaware of the problem, then not sure whether I was trying to bear off or tack again, did not know whether to trim or slack sheets. All in a tangle, I did clear the wheel spokes enough to whirl her into the wind and tack. I didn't look over the side to see if I could see bottom, nor did I look at the ledge, but it was quite close enough. Hugh observed that it was good for the circulation to be scared half to death once in a while. We jibed over and went home.

In spite of having come very close to beating *Dorothy Elizabeth*'s brains out on a ledge we had avoided a thousand times, it was a good sail. We now had confidence that she was a good sea boat, could go anywhere coastwise, and, with a little more ballast, handle any kind of summer weather she might meet. I knew, too, that we had a boat again, that no longer were we shorebound or guests on other people's boats. We had done what we set out to do two years before when I had called Ralph and said, "Let's build the little schooner."

## The End

*Dorothy Elizabeth* under way at last

# EPILOGUE

## IS IT WORTH IT?

THE ANSWER IS AN UNEQUIVOCAL YES. IT HAS BEEN worth it. It is worth it. It will be worth it.

It has been worth it because it has drawn together a subtle community of people who have united to produce a beautiful little schooner, a work of art, a strong, able vessel capable of standing the strains of old Ocean. She's beautiful to look at, strong enough to take your life in her hands. This community includes all those who have had a part, from Ralph Stanley, who conceived her and who created the shop that built her, through all who built her hull and all those at Frank Luke's yard who cared for her, worked on her, met her sudden emergencies, and "stopped by" to give advice and lend a hand. It includes everyone in Nat Wilson's sail loft who took a stitch in her sails. Our own family is part of this community, too, from my brother Don who was carpenter, rigger, ballast lumper, and gopher boy and who piped her into Linekin Bay, to sisters, sons, grandchildren, nieces and nephews, and cousins who gave time, support, and good wishes. And there are so many others—from those that gave the flag at her peak to those who provided the ribbons on the bottle that christened her. She has been worth it to us to be a part of this community.

She is worth it to us. We who were shorebound are now afloat. Captain and mate, we are crew of a vessel. We are responsible for her; she is part of our lives; she tells us who we are.

She will be worth it, for we will share her with many people. At sea, under sail in a small boat, especially a small wooden boat, one touches Earth's elemental forces: sun and stars, wind and wave, salt water, tide, and rain and fog. We are made of these things. They are in blood and brain and heart. Aboard *Dorothy Elizabeth* we can share these, and many others can share after us.

She has been a delight to build, is a delight to look at and a delight to sail.

I speak of her as if she were a person. In our minds she assumes a character, a character partly inspired by her names, for our mothers were much loved. Part of her character is inspired by the skill and care that went into her construction. Part of her character comes from the interest and admiration of those who saw her launched, who see her sailing, and those who have hailed us in store and post office: "How's the new boat coming?" And part of her character comes from her responsiveness, her apparent pleasure in pressing to windward, her liveliness on a reach, her discomfort at being half full of water after 9 inches of rain. Part of her character is inborn, inexplicable, mystical, magical. It is worth it to have created such a being.

Is it worth it? One cannot answer this question satisfactorily in words. The answer is more than words can say. Our son Robert said it after our first sail offshore:

# Joy

IT WAS LATE October in the afternoon. The fall sun shed a cool metallic reflection over the water to the west. *Dorothy Elizabeth* lay over and the lee rail dipped into a gray cold sea. The little 28-foot schooner set to work going to windward in earnest. Every part of the rig right to the main topsail was taut and humming to the strain of a building southwest wind. Just off to leeward was Fisherman Island. In the height of summer it is green and gold and glistens like an island meadow. But the green and gold had been replaced by a soft gray where ledge pushed through the brown of old grass and bushes gone to seed for the winter. My father spun the wheel over, and his new schooner turned on her heel and pushed her bow through the wind onto the port tack. Fisherman Island was now behind us, and the bowsprit pointed right down the sun's path. "Sailing down the sun" is my term for a port-tack hitch in the late afternoon. It was blowing cold, and the wind carried a heft to it that's not there in summer. We needed another half mile before we could fetch by the ledge off Fisherman, and with the low water would need to give it a bit more berth than usual.

*Dorothy Elizabeth* felt the shoulder of seas marching in from the Gulf of Maine. An offshore sea feels different than a coastal chop. The deep heave of each hump was more than a wave. It was a message from the open ocean with weight, and power, and authority. Each sea that rolled under her, and every gust that pushed the lee waterway a bit deeper, meant another few yards to windward. *Dorothy Elizabeth* settled down to do her work, and she did it well. After 10 minutes we tacked again and could see the ledge off the end of the island just under the lee bow. We could fetch, and once around, could bear off and run for home.

Aboard was my father at the wheel, his roommate from high school—an old saltwater ally—my mother, and me. Dad was on his new boat, just to windward of the harbor islands, and open ocean ahead. His friend and family stood ready to trim a sheet or snug up a halyard. He was 18 months out from a critical medical disaster that had been averted only by modern medicine and ancient grace. He had been unable to lift his head from the pillow and now was driving his new schooner into the teeth of a smoky southwest breeze at the end of a short fall day. The memories of long months of rehabilitation were slipping away like the smooth wake silently sliding by the curved transom of *Dorothy*

*Elizabeth*'s stern. Just being there was a gift. Joy's companion was gratitude. There are some things "they" (whoever "they" are) can't take away from you. That moment is one of them. During quiet seconds of reflection in the midst of hectic winter days, the Joy of that late fall afternoon is as permanent as anything ever can be in this life.

# GLOSSARY

**adze**  A tool like an axe with its blade turned 90 degrees and rounded in. It has a twisted handle and is used to shape a timber.

**aneurysm**  A main blood vessel bursts at a weak place and badly upsets the body's circulatory system. More complete details are available in medical texts. The affliction can be fatal.

**awash**  Level with the water; full of water.

**azimuth**  (1) The bearing of a heavenly body in degrees. (2) An instrument for measuring azimuths accurately.

**back**  To push a sail to windward so it pushes the boat backward. A backed sail turns the boat's bow away from the backed sail.

**ballast**  Weight carried to help prevent a boat from tipping too much.

**bare poles**  Showing no sail at all, usually because of stress of weather.

**bark**  A vessel square-rigged on its two or three forward masts and with a gaff-headed sail on the after mast. USCG *Eagle* is a bark.

**batten**  A long, thin piece of wood.

**beam reach**  A course 90 degrees from the direction of the wind. Some fun!

**beam trawler**  A fishing vessel that tows a net along the ocean floor.

**bear off**  To turn the boat away from the direction from which the wind is blowing.

**beard line**  The line drawn on the plan and on the stem to show where the inside of the planking touches the stem.

**beat**  To sail against the wind by sailing first with sails on one side and then on the other.

**becket**  The metal fitting on a block to which one end of the rope is attached.

**before the wind**  A vessel sailing before the wind is moving in the direction in which the wind is blowing.

**belaying pin**  A wooden peg that fits into a hole in the pinrail, to which a halyard is tied or belayed.

**bend on**  Usually of sails. To attach to the spars. In other cases, to attach, as to bend on an anchor.

**bevel**  (1) Angle. The outside edge of a plank is beveled to take the caulking. (2) A bevel is a tool for transferring an angle.

**bilge**  The space at the very bottom of the inside of the boat, under the cabin floor and under the engine. Unless frequently cleaned, it can get pretty awful.

**bilge clamp**  A timber bolted to the frames on the inside of the boat about halfway from the keel to the rail at the turn of the bilge. It helps to stiffen the whole structure.

**bilge water**  Water that collects in the bilge.

**binnacle**  A stand wherein sits the compass.

**bitt**  A stout, vertical timber going down through the deck and firmly stepped below. It is designed to take heavy strains. The bitter end of an anchor line is usually made fast to the bitt below the deck, lest one lose anchor chain and line.

**bitter end**  Of an anchor line, the end which is attached to the bitt below the deck. The end which is not used. Metaphorically, the very last. Not to be confused with the sense of taste.

**block**  A nautical pulley.

**bobstay**  A wire from the bowsprit to the stem to prevent the bowsprit from bending upward.

**bolt rope**  The rope sewed around the edge of a sail to protect and strengthen it.

**boom**  Spar at the bottom of a sail.

**bosun's chair**   A board with holes in it through which is rove a rope sling. One sits on the board to be hoisted aloft. It is like a child's swing.

**bowsprit**   A spar projecting from the bow of the boat.

**bow thruster**   A vessel with a bow thruster has a pump or propeller in an orifice in the side of her bow so that her bow can be pushed sideways. Common on big vessels but unusual in small yachts.

**bridge deck**   The place where the deck runs across the boat from rail to rail between cockpit and cabin. In *Dorothy Elizabeth*, the mainmast is stepped through it.

**broad reach**   A vessel on a broad reach has the wind between 90° and 160° from her bow. Usually a boat's fastest point of sailing.

**bulkhead**   Wall.

**bullet block**   A small single block, usually bronze, with the cheeks extended and joined. Much used for jibsheets.

**bung**   A wooden peg set over the head of a screw to make a neat finish.

**burgee**   A triangular flag usually bearing the logo of a yacht club.

**butt**   (1) The big end of a timber. (2) The place where two planks come together end to end on the side of a boat. A butt is usually backed by a butt block.

**buttock lines**   On a plan, lines where a plane perpendicular to the waterline and parallel to the centerline of the boat would intersect the hull.

**cabin house**   A structure erected on the deck to provide head-room in the cabin.

**carvel**   A method of planking in which the planks fit smoothly edge to edge.

**caught down**   Tangled up below the surface so it cannot be raised. Said of a mooring, an anchor line, a lobster trap, or a fish line.

**caulk**  To drive cotton or oakum into a seam and fill the seam with seam compound.

**centerboard**  A board that can be raised or lowered through a slot in the keel.

**centerboard trunk**  The box in which the centerboard moves. It must extend from the keel to above the waterline.

**chainplates**  Metal strips bolted to the hull, to which the shrouds are attached.

**check**  (1) v. Said of a timber. To crack along the grain because the outside dries and shrinks while the inside is still green and damp. (2) n. Such a crack.

**cheek block**  A block that can be screwed to a spar with the sheave parallel to the spar. A topsail sheet or a reef pennant might be led through it.

**chop**  A short, steep sea.

**clamp**  A C-shaped piece of metal with a screw in one arm to hold two pieces of wood together temporarily. See also *deck clamp* and *bilge clamp*.

**cleat**  In *Dorothy Elizabeth*, a narrow piece of wood, longer on top than on the bottom, screwed edgeways on the deck. A rope can be wound around it and thus made fast, yet be quickly released.

**clew**  The after lower corner of a sail.

**clove hitch**  A knot in which a line is passed twice around a fixed object and both ends brought out between the turns in opposite directions. It will not slip up or down the object, but if made with nylon rope and subject to great strain, it is almost impossible to release.

**close reach**  Sailing at an angle a little less than 90 degrees to the wind.

**coaming**  A vertical plank surrounding a cockpit or hatch to keep water out.

**cockpit**  A low place in the deck near the stern where people sit.

**come-along**  A hand winch by which one small human can exert unbelievable force.

**companionway**  Hatch at the after end of the cabin house, giving access to the cabin.

**cotter pin**  A split pin which can be passed through a hole and the ends spread to prevent its coming out.

**counter**  The stern of the finished boat on which the name is usually painted.

**cringle**  A brass eye, doughnut shaped and grooved on the outside, worked into the bolt rope of a sail to take a reef earing. Pronounced *crinkle*.

**cutter**  A sloop with the mast two-fifths of the way from the bow, usually carrying a bowsprit and two jibs.

**deadeye**  A block of hardwood with three holes. One deadeye is attached to the chainplate and another spliced into the lower end of a shroud. A lanyard is run through the holes and hauled tight to support the mast.

**deadwood**  The part of the boat just above the keel in the stern where the boat is not hollow but solid wood through and through; the part below the bottom plank.

**deck clamp**  A timber running fore and aft inside the boat and bolted to the inside of the frames. The deck beams rest on it. It gives the boat longitudinal stiffness.

**deck iron**  A ring of galvanized iron or stainless steel set in the deck, through which a stovepipe is led. It is grooved on the top to hold water so the deck will not scorch.

**depth sounder**  An electronic device for measuring the depth of water under a boat.

**dinghy**  A small boat used as a tender for a yacht.

**dogs**  (1) Metal devices like belt buckles that fit around a frame and will slide down but not up. Used in planking.
(2) A wingnut or lever to force a door or portlight hard against a gasket to make it watertight.

**double head rig**  Carrying two jibs.

**downhaul**  A rope to haul a sail down. It is sometimes reluctant to come down quickly.

**drag**  The angle of the keel to the waterline.

**drift**  n. A rod driven into a hole too small for it. Once in, it is immovable. It is used to fasten timbers together in places where the end of the rod cannot be reached to put a nut on it. v. To put in a drift. Two timbers are drifted together. v. To float, unattached and out of control.

**ear**  A block of wood screwed to the mast, grooved on top to accommodate the wire which rests on it. Its purpose is to prevent the wire from sliding down the mast.

**earing**  A rope used in reefing passed through an eye in the luff and one in the leach, each of which must be tied down to the boom.

**ease**  To slack away a bit.

**ensign**  Our national flag. Old Glory. Or the flag of any nation.

**eyebolt**  A metal eye with a threaded shaft with a washer and nut.

**fair**  (1) v. To eliminate bumps, humps, or hollows. (2) adj. Smooth, even. Said of a curve or curved plank.

**fairlead**  A doughnut of wood or plastic to guide a rope.

**false timber**  A short piece of oak lying vertically under the deck between the planking and the deck clamp with a lip to catch under the deck clamp. The chainplate is bolted through it.

**fetch**  (1) n. The wind or sea has a long fetch when it is unobstructed by land. (2) v. To pass to windward of an obstruction, ledge, or buoy.

**fid**  A conical spike of polished hardwood about a foot long and an inch in diameter.

**fisherman staysail**  A quadrilateral sail set between the masts of a schooner. One corner to the top of the mainmast, one to the top of the foremast, the tack to the foremast, and the sheet aft to the quarter.

**fitting out**   Making ready for sea. Includes rigging, provisioning, and anything else necessary.

**flake**   v. To fold a lowered sail accordion-fashion on the boom if it is too stiff to furl. Also to lay out rope or chain for running clear.

**flasher**   A buoy bearing a flashing light.

**floor timbers**   Timbers inside the boat attached to the keel that run across the boat and fasten to the planks on each side to hold the two halves of the boat together at the bottom.

**fo'c's'le**   The living space for the crew, usually in the bow.

**Fochabers ginger cake**   Prepared from a recipe originated in the town of Fochabers in northern Scotland from which Duncans emigrated to America. The secret recipe is not easily obtained, but you can try.

**foresail**   A gaff-headed sail set on the foremast.

**forestay**   A wire leading from high on the foremast to the bowsprit to prevent the foremast from falling aft. The forestaysail hoists on this stay.

**foul**   Overgrown with weed or barnacles, twisted, tangled, rocky, undesirable, bad.

**frame**   A timber attached to the keel on the inside of the planking and extending upwards to the deck, analogous to a rib in bird, beast, or fish.

**freeboard**   Height of the hull above the water.

**Friendship sloop**   A sloop of the type used by Maine fishermen in the early years of the twentieth century, characterized by a sharp bow, a width about one-third of the length, a flat run, and a gaff rig.

**furl**   To roll a lowered sail neatly up inside itself.

**gaff**   (1) The spar at the top of a quadrilateral sail.
(2) A hook on a stick for lifting things out of the water.

**gaff bridle**   A short piece of wire with a splice in each end.

The splices are slipped over the gaff and held apart by wooden chocks. Its purpose is to distribute the strain of the peak halyard along the gaff.

**gaff jaws**   The pieces bolted to the sides of the gaff to hold it to the mast. Ideally, they will be made of wood with a natural crook to the grain so the jaw can lie at right angles to the mast when the sail is hoisted and the gaff peaked up.

**gaff topsail**   A triangular sail set above the gaff.

**galley**   Kitchen.

**gangway**   A bridge from wharf to float.

**garboard**   The bottom plank next to the keel.

**gold-plater**   An elegantly appointed and finely finished yacht. Cost is no consideration.

**GPS**   Global Positioning System. A tiny radio and computer that receives messages from passing satellites and announces your position, course, speed, and other relevant data.

**grommet**   A doughnut of rope.

**gudgeon**   A strap to hold the rudder to the boat.

**half-model**   A model of half of a boat cut lengthwise from bow to stern. It is used as a means of designing a boat, for it can be taken apart and enlarged to life size.

**halyard**   A rope used to hoist a sail.

**head**   A marine toilet.

**headroom**   Height in which to stand up in the cabin (full headroom is about 6 feet).

**headsails**   Jib and staysail. Sails forward of the mast.

**herringbone**   A kind of sailmaker's stitch used to join two pieces of cloth so they will not overlap. It is better than the stitch used to sew up a baseball, but it does the same thing.

**hog**   To droop at bow and stern.

**horn timber**   Timber on top of the after deadwood, projecting aft to hold up the stern.

**hull speed**   One-and-a-half times the square root of a boat's waterline length.

**jackline** A line running alternately through eyes in the luff of a sail and the hoops or rings that hold the sail to the mast or stay. When the sail comes down, the jackline goes slack, making the sail easier to furl.

**jackstay** In *Dorothy Elizabeth*, a line from the point where the topmast touches the top of the mainmast to a small tackle at the foot of the mainmast. A cringle in the luff of the topsail is attached to it, rides up on it, and pulls the luff of the topsail tight when the tackle is set up.

**jib** A triangular sail set on a stay forward of the mast.

**jibe** To turn the boat so far away from the wind that the wind hits the after edge of the sail and slams the sail across the boat. To jibe is to turn the boat away from the wind; to tack is to turn through the eye of the wind.

**jumbo** The Gloucester fisherman's name for the big forestaysail on a Gloucester schooner.

**kedge** An anchor of the traditional shape.

**keel** (1) The main timber at the bottom of the boat to which frames, stem, sternpost, and floor timbers are fastened. (2) The heavy piece of iron or lead ballast bolted to the wooden keel.

**ketch** A sailboat with two masts, the after mast being shorter than the other and stepped forward of the rudder post.

**knot** A rate of speed equal to 1 nautical mile (6,080 feet) per hour.

**lanyard** The rope run through the holes in a deadeye to tighten the shrouds and support the mast.

**lay** Noun or verb. Twist.

**leach** The after edge of a sail.

**lee** The side away from the wind. To be in the lee of something is to be sheltered by it.

**lee shore** A shore against which the wind is blowing, a dangerous situation, imminent shipwreck.

**leeward** Pronounced loo'ard. The direction toward which the wind is blowing. Down the wind.

**leeway** Slipping sideways down the wind.

**lintel** The timber over the top of a door.

**lofting** The procedure for enlarging a boat's plans to life size on the floor. Patterns are made from these lines.

**log** (1) A book in which is kept a record of the voyage. (2) A device for measuring speed through the water.

**logy** Sluggish. Disinclined to move quickly.

**luff** (1) n. The forward edge of a sail. (2) v. To head toward the wind so the luff of the sail shakes, spills the wind, and slows the boat.

**mainsail** The large sail aft of the aftermost mast on a sloop or schooner.

**make fast** Fasten. Tie tightly so it will not come loose.

**Marconi** Jib headed, triangular, as opposed to gaff headed or quadrilateral.

**marline** Small line, tarred string, two stranded, laid left handed and wound around a wire splice to protect it.

**marlinespike** A tapered steel spike about 10 inches long, the end of which is flattened and its edges sharpened. It is used principally to open the strands of wire rigging.

**masthead** Top of the mast.

**mast hoop** An oak or ash hoop that encircles a mast and to which a sail is lashed.

**maul** A sledgehammer, sharp at one end.

**mitre** In a triangular sail, a seam from clew to luff. The panels on top and bottom of the sail meet at the mitre at an angle.

**mizzen** The after mast or sail on a ketch or yawl. Always smaller than the forward sail.

**mold** Of a wooden boat, a cross section of the boat to the inside of the plank. It is made of light boards and straddles the keel to give shape to the ribbands and planks that will later be bent around it. After the boat is planked, the molds are removed.

**mooring**  A rock or heavy anchor with a chain and buoy to which one can tie up.

**mouse**  To lash a shackle pin or hook in place with marline or wire.

**nautical mile**  6,080 feet, 1 minute of latitude.

**on the wind**  Sailing with the wind forward of the beam as close to the direction from which the wind is coming as possible.

**painter**  A rope attached to the bow of a small boat to tie it to a float, wharf, or larger boat.

**parceled**  Wrapped with canvas, said of a wire.

**parral beads**  Wooden beads strung on a line between the jaws of a boom or a gaff to prevent the spar from jumping away from the mast. They also prevent the line from catching on the mast as the spar goes up or down.

**part**  v. Break.

**party boat**  A boat used to carry passengers for hire.

**pass the ball**  To help a rigger by handing the ball of marline around the wire being served so the rigger can keep both hands on the serving mallet.

**pay out scope**  Slacken the anchor rope so there will be more rope between the boat and the anchor.

**pay the seams**  To fill the seam over the caulking with white lead, putty, or seam compound. Old-timers used hot pitch.

**peak halyard**  The halyard that hoists the after end of a gaff.

**peapod**  A small rowboat pointed at each end. It is often towed behind a larger boat.

**pennant**  (1) A small triangular flag. (2) (Properly pendant) A short piece of line. A reef pennant for reefing, a mooring pennant for attaching a vessel to a mooring buoy.

**pillow block** A block of wood between the jaws of a gaff, curved to fit the mast and pivoted on a bolt so it will bear on the mast whether the gaff is peaked up or not.

**pinch line** A line to be slacked off under strain to prevent anything from falling or sliding too rapidly.

**pinrail** A wooden bar lashed to the shrouds on each side of the boat. Vertical holes are bored in it to accommodate belaying pins.

**points** The traditional 32 markings around the compass card. A point is 11¼°. To name the points in order is to, box the compass."

**quarter** Either side of the stern.

**quarter wave** A wave that an ill-designed boat drags around after her wherever she goes. Any boat will generate one at hull speed or greater.

**rabbet** A groove in a timber into which a plank fits.

**rabbet line** The line, usually shown on the plan, where the outside of the plank meets the stem, keel, or deadwood.

**rail breeze** A wind strong enough to heel a boat to her rail.

**reef** The sail to be reefed is fitted with a row of reef points parallel to the boom and with a brass eye, a cringle, at each end of the row. First, the tack earing is passed through the forward cringle and tied down to the boom. The sail is then stretched tightly along the line of the reef points, pulled aft, and tied down by the clew earing passed through the after cringle. Then the gathered sail is tied up by tying the ends of the reef points together between the sail and the boom.

**reef points** Small short lines passing through a sail. The ends are tied together under the sail in reefing.

**rib** See *frame*. The usual term is frame or timber.

**ribbands** Strips of wood about an inch square, running fore and aft and bent around the molds. The frames are bent to the inside of the ribbands, clamped there, and nailed temporarily. When the boat is planked, the ribbands are removed.

**rode** Anchor line.

**roll-up jib** Properly called a Roller Furling System, it is a jib with a wire luff rigged to wind itself up around the luff wire when a line on a reel at the tack of the sail is pulled, and to unwind when that line is released and the sheet is pulled. Sometimes called a geriatric jib because no old man has to go out on the bowsprit.

**rudder post** The timber to which the rudder is attached. It is turned by the tiller or wheel.

**run** The after part of the boat's underbody where the water leaves her.

**running lights** A red light for the port side, a green light for the starboard, a white light showing aft, and another showing forward.

**running rigging** The ropes used to haul sails up or pull them in.

**schooner** A two-masted sailing vessel with the aftermost mast taller than the forward mast.

**scupper** A hole in the toe rail to let water run off the deck. Also a pipe leading overboard from the floor of a self-bailing cockpit.

**sea** A wave or series of waves.

**served** Wound very tightly with marline.

**serving** A winding of marline around a wire splice.

**serving mallet** A grooved mallet used to wind a serving tightly.

**shackle** A U-shaped piece of metal with a pin across the horns. The pin goes through one horn and is usually threaded into the other.

**sheave** The wheel inside a block.

**sheer** The curve of the deck from bow to stern.

**sheerline**  The line of the sheer as shown on a plan.

**sheet**  The rope that pulls a sail in across the boat.

**Shipmate stove**  A cast iron stove burning coal, wood, briquets, or anything inflammable.

**shoal draft**  Requiring little water in which to float.

**shrouds**  Wires supporting a spar from side to side.

**shutter**  The last plank to be put on the boat.

**sloop**  A sailboat with one mast and one or more jibs in front of it.

**snub**  To take a turn of a line around a post, cleat, or piling to prevent its running out.

**sole**  (1) Floor, either cockpit or cabin. (2) The bottom of a carpenter's plane.

**spar**  A stick or pole on which a sail is set.

**spar ironwork**  Metal bands and straps that fit around the spars to which various ropes and wires are attached. Must be made to fit a specific boat.

**spiling**  Designing and cutting a board to fit the place where it must be as a plank in a vessel.

**splice**  To interweave the strands of a rope or wire in such a way as to make a loop in the rope or wire, or to join two ropes or wires together.

**spinnaker**  A big balloon of a sail made of very light cloth. It is set forward of the mast for running downwind.

**springstay**  The stay connecting the tops of the two masts of a schooner.

**square drift**  A course made good of 90 degrees to the wind.

**standing part**  The part of the rope or wire that takes the main strain and into which the strands of the other part are tucked to make an eye splice.

**standing rigging**  The wires supporting the mast.

**starboard tack**  With the wind coming over the starboard (right) side. A vessel on the starboard tack has the right of way over a vessel on the port tack.

**stay** A wire to prevent the mast from falling forward or back.

**staysail** The inner jib if there are two.

**stem** The heavy timber at the bow of the boat to which the planking is fastened. It is bolted to the keel.

**step** (1) v. To put a mast erect in its proper place.
(2) n. A timber bridging several floor timbers with a socket into which the butt of a mast fits.

**stern bearing** A bearing through which the propellor shaft goes out through the stern.

**strap** A loop of rope or wire often used to go around a spar.

**strongback** A board arching from bow to stern over the molds during construction to hold the molds down tightly on the keel.

**stuffing box** A device to prevent water from coming into a boat around a shaft such as a rudder post or propellor shaft. Usually a hollow nut packed with flax.

**sway hook** A bronze hook with a long, threaded shank installed on the deck under a pinrail. A halyard is led under the hook and up to the belaying pin.

**swaged** Spliced mechanically by slipping a soft metal sleeve over the two parts to be spliced and passing it through a machine that squeezes it very tightly to both parts.

**tack** (1) n. The forward lower corner of a sail. (2) v. With the wind blowing on one side of the sail, to turn the boat into the wind and around so the wind fills the sail on the other side.

**tack downhaul** A tackle under the forward end of the boom at the tack of the sail, to pull the tack down and stretch the luff tight along the mast.

**tack earing** A rope tying an eye in the sail down to the tack of the sail. Used in reefing.

**tackle** Two or more blocks or pulleys with rope running between them in such a way as to gain a mechanical advantage. Pronounced "tayckle."

**taffrail**   The rail around the stern of a boat.

**thimble**   a horseshoe-shaped piece of metal with the horns bent together and grooved on the outside. Used to line the eye of a splice to prevent it from collapsing and to avoid chafe.

**throat halyard**   The halyard that hoists the forward end of the gaff. Usually a double and a single block.

**thrum mat**   A mat woven of old rope. It is installed at the end of a traveler to prevent the sheet blocks from beating on the deck.

**tiller**   A stick attached to the rudder post by which the boat is steered.

**toerail**   A low rail at the outer edge of the deck running the length of the boat to brace a foot against and to keep valuable things from rolling overboard.

**topmast**   A light spar attached to the top of a lower mast on which a light sail can be set.

**topmast stay**   The wire from the top of the main topmast to the top of the foremast.

**topping lift**   A rope from the end of a boom through a block high on the mast and then to the deck. Its purpose is to support the boom when the sail is not set.

**traveler**   A metal bar running athwartships to which a sheet block is attached.

**Turnabout**   An 8-foot plywood craft, usually fitted with only one sail, originally designed by one Turner. An inexpensive craft in which children learn to sail.

**up-helm**   To bear off, to swing the boat away from the wind. With a tiller, one pulls the tiller toward the high or windward side of the boat to accomplish this.

**warp**   (1) v. To pull a vessel by a rope attached to something solid like a wharf. (2) n. The said rope.

**waterline(s)** (1) Line where the water rests when the boat floats. (2) On a plan, lines where a plane parallel to the water would intersect the side of the boat.

**ways** Heavy timbers laid parallel to each other from the shore into deep water. A vessel in a cradle slides down the ways into the water and floats off the cradle.

**weather bow** The side of the boat forward of the mast which is toward the wind.

**wheel** (1) A device for steering the boat. (2) A propellor.

**wing and wing** Sailing with the mainsail on one side and the foresail on the other. Possible only with the wind well aft.

**whipping** A winding of sail twine sewed to the end of a rope to prevent its unraveling.

**white lead** Basic lead carbonate and linseed oil used to make paint and as a paste to pay seams, and to set fittings and bungs. It is poisonous, now illegal, and almost unavailable.

**windward** Toward the direction from which the wind is blowing.

**winter stick** In our case, a 6 by 6 timber chained to the mooring chain. If it is frozen into the ice, it will lean over and pull out if the ice moves and not be cut off.

**yaw** To pursue an unsteady course.

**yawl** A sailboat with two masts, the after mast being shorter than the other and stepped aft of the rudder post.

# TIME LINE

**July 1996**   We decided to give *Eastward* to our son Robert and get a smaller boat.

**September 10**   We talked with Ralph Stanley about a schooner.

**September 12**   End of our last cruise on *Eastward*.

**September 21**   We drove to Southwest Harbor to see the first drawing of *Dorothy Elizabeth*.

**September 30**   We called Ralph to say, "Let's build the little schooner."

**October 11**   We had our last sail as owners of *Eastward*.

**October 22**   We saw the revised drawing of *Dorothy Elizabeth*.

**November 8**   We saw a computer image of *Dorothy Elizabeth*.

**November 10**   I tried to cut a gaff jaw out of a big tree adrift.

**November 16**   We went to Portland to talk about engines.

**December 3**   Nat Wilson agreed to build a suit of sails.

**January 8, 1997**   Lofting was done and patterns made.

**February 3**   We watched Ralph cutting out the deadwood.

**March 3**   The deadwood was bolted together.

**March 14**   I started the first wire splice.

**March 15**   We saw the backbone and stem set up.

**March 27**   The molds were in place and frames bent in.

**March 31**   The first garboard was fastened in.

**April 7**   We saw the boat about half planked.

**April 16**   We had a "shutter party."

**April 21**   The side decks were framed, floor timbers in, and we "went aboard" for the first time.

**April 23**   The Crash

**April 29**   The hull was smoothed, caulking started, and false frames for the chainplates were installed.

**May 1**   The caulking was nearly done, the engine hanging from a chain fall waiting for the beds. Stuffing box in and shelf going in.

**May 8**   Mary, Donald, and Joyce drove to Southwest Harbor and reported caulking done and the deck framed.

**May 21**   Donald got a sample portlight from J. J.

**June 12**   I came home from the hospital.

**June 23**   Bob and Alec brought *Eastward* to our mooring.

**July 3**   I resumed splicing standing rigging.

**July 26**   Frank Luke agreed to take in *Dorothy Elizabeth* for the winter, step masts, and launch her when the time came.

**August 8**   We drove to Southwest Harbor, went aboard, and saw the cabin sides in place and the rudder and steering gear installed.

**August 10**   We had a sail as guests in *Eastward*.

**August 20**   The top of *Dorothy Elizabeth*'s house was on.

**September 19**   Ralph brought the spars to Frank's yard.

**September 23**   We visited the "bee lady," continued to Southwest Harbor, and watched Richard establish the waterline.

**October 8**   Nat Wilson came in to talk specifically about sails.

**October 16**   *Dorothy Elizabeth* was towed across Southwest Harbor and brought to Frank's on a trailer.

**October 18**   Homecoming Party.

**October 20**   Douglas Day made a set of gaff jaws.

**October 28**   We saw *Dorothy Elizabeth*'s mainsail laid out.

**October 31**   I watched Jinny cut out our topsail.

**November 21**   We sat in the cockpit with Donald and planned the deck layout.

**February 7, 1998**   Finished splicing the lower standing rigging.

**March 2**   I took the masthead fittings to John Luke for him to make bails for the springstay and topmast stays.

**March 31**  Nat Wilson finished up the first wire strap for me.

**April 5**  I finished the last of the standing rigging.

**April 22**  Keith found the iron in the rock for the float.

**June 7**  I finished the fore gaff and took it to the yard.

**June 17**  Donald and I bolted down the handrail.

**July 10**  I went mate on *Eastward* with Capt. Alec, Stefan, and Natasha.

**July 29**  I tarred and painted the rigging. Frank discovered the sway hook.

**August 11**  Frank started on engine controls and bilge pump.

**August 12**  We took the main gaff and both booms to the yard.

**August 15**  We poured beeswax into the checks in the masts.

**August 18**  We started carpentry work on the masts.

**August 21**  With much help, we painted the spars.

**August 23**  We installed cleats.

**August 25**  Alec carved the document numbers into the side of the house.

**August 25**  We went to Bill Page's shop in Cushing for hardware.

**August 27**  We started to hang rigging on the spars.

**August 28**  We drove to Hamilton Marine for more hardware.

**September 4**  We rigged the bowsprit.

**September 8**  Mary broke her arm and wrenched her shoulder.

**September 9**  We hung the running rigging.

**September 10**  Jon Marsh painted *Dorothy Elizabeth*'s name.

**September 12**  We stepped the topmast.

**September 14**  Log and depthsounder installed by Bob Ayers.

**September 16**  Frank, and others, stepped the masts.

**September 19**  LAUNCHING PARTY and first sail under foresail alone.

**September 26**  We bent the mainsail.

**October 4**  Our first real sail.

**October 17**  Bill Tefft took pictures of *Dorothy Elizabeth* under sail. Ralph and Marion were aboard.

**October 18**  Our first sail in the big deep ocean.

**October 23**  We laid up *Dorothy Elizabeth* for the winter.

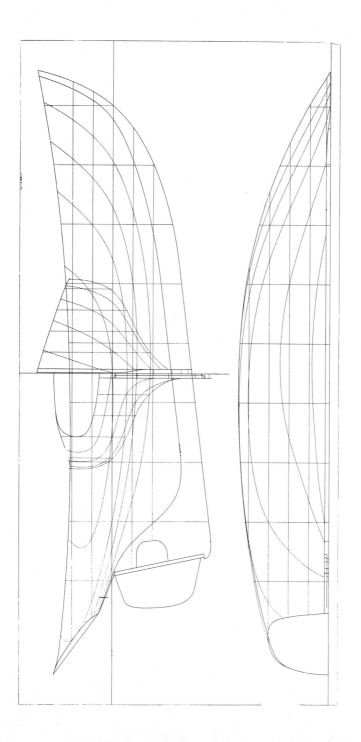

## A

*Adventure* (schooner), 55
Alden, John, 35
anchor, plow, 179
anchor bitt, 108, 116
anchor chain, 110
anchor line, 110, 196
anchoring on a lee shore, 196
Andrea, boat carpenter, 20-21, 90-93, 97-105
*Appledore* (schooner), 199
Ayers, Bob, 185, 187

## B

backbone assembly, 71-75
lofting, 15, 67, 69-71
deadwood, 71-75
keel rabbet, 98-102
lead keel, 73
oak for, 35, 71
stem, 15, 69-71
wood keel, 72-74, 98-102
Bader, Stefan and Natasha, 130-33
ballast placement/trim, 11, 33, 199
Bar Harbor, 56-57
bare hull, 28, 48
Bath Iron Works, 78-79, 148
becalmed, 54-56
beeswax, for filling checks in spars, 139-40, 175-76
bilge pump, 150-51
bitts, 108, 116
blocks, 66, 178, 183-84
boat:
  naming, 28-30
  painting (color scheme), 27-28
  sailing herself, 65
  *see also* wooden boat
Booth Bay, 39, 199-204
Boothbay Harbor, 39, 199
Butler, Farnham and Gladys, 103

## C

Casco Passage, Blue Hill Bay, 17, 54
caulking, 27, 41, 118-120
C-clamps, spinning, 90
cedar, Eastern white, 35
chainplates, 117-118, 188
Chalmers, Dan, 143, 146
clipper ship, 32
  *see also Flying Scud;
  Red Jacket*
cockpit:
  deep, 23, 33, 108, 138
  self-bailing, 23, 26
Coffin, Dave, 165
color for a boat, 27-28
compass, 157-61
  adjusting/correction, 160-61
  card marked in points and degrees, 158-61
*Constitution, USS*,
  reconstruction of, 64, 68
Coulen, Tim, rigger, 77-78
Cranberry Islands, 88-89
Cruising Club of America, 135-36, 137
*Cruising Guide to the New England Coast*, 32-33, 136, 187

**D**

Dauphinee, A., 66, 103, 184

Day, Douglas (Doug), 149, 169-70

deck clamps and bilge clamps, 108-9

*Dictator* (sloop), 68

docking under sail, 50-53, 55, 128, 129

*Dorothy* (shoal-draft schooner), 22, 30, 31

*Dorothy* (sloop), 30, 51, 64-65, 137, 150-51, 196

*Dorothy Elizabeth* (schooner):
anchor and quarter bitts, 108, 116
anchor chain, 110
backbone assembly, 35, 71-75, 88, 98-102
ballast, 11, 30, 199
boom jaws, 173
cabin, 11, 108, 138-39
chainplates, 117-18, 188
cockpit, 23, 33, 108, 138
deck clamps, bilge clamps, and floor timbers, 108-9, 111
design of, 21-25, 27-28, 32-35, 45-46, 48-49
double head rig, 34-35, 46, 48
engine, 49, 50-58
fittings and hardware, 87-88, 120-22, 165-66, 177-79
flooded, 200-201, 207
fore hatch, 110, 138, 141, 196
frames, 35, 90-93

gaff jaws, 59, 149-50, 169-71, 173
gaff main topsail, 46, 48, 151
house and companionway, 164-65
jib, roll-up, 34, 46, 189-90, 192, 198-99
launching, 182-83, 192-95
lofting/laying down the lines, 15, 67, 69-71
mooring, hauling, and storage, 60, 62-63, 137-38, 148
naming of, 28-30
planking, 35, 40, 96-105
pre-launch crises, 189-91
running rigging, 50, 178, 182-91, 192-99
sailing, 196-205, 207-9
sails, 34, 46, 49, 63-64, 142, 151-54, 189-90, 192, 197, 198-99
shutter party, 103-5
side decks, 107-8
spars, 49, 63, 139-40, 175-77, 180-81, 184, 187-88
standing rigging, 49, 50, 77-86, 102, 166-69
staysail, 46
steering gear, 64-66
stepping the masts, 184, 187-88
trailering and Homecoming, 142-46
wheel box, 138, 141

Dumont, Melanie, 139-40

Duncan, Alec, 17, 125-34, 193, 196-97

Duncan, Donald, 103, 113, 120, 156, 164, 184, 189-91, 193-95, 198-200, 206

Duncan, Joyce, 103

Duncan, Mark, 193, 196-97

Duncan, Mary Chandler, 11, 15-16, 45, 47, 120-23, 182, 184-85, 193-95, 199
  poems of, 112-13, 114, 140on Roger's aneurysm and recovery, 112-13, 114

Duncan, Robert (Bob), 17, 18, 47, 125, 193, 201-3
  on sailing *Dorothy Elizabeth*, 207-9

Duncan, Roger F.
  aneurysm of the aorta and recovery, 112-15, 116-17, 120, 125, 135-36
  *Cruising Guide to the New England Coast*, 32-33, 136, 187
  as *Eastward* observer/passenger/mate, 126-34
  splicing wire rigging, 16, 77-86, 102

Duncan, Roger S., 175

**E**

*Eastward* (Friendship sloop), 15-17, 126-28
  engine, 49, 57
  half-model of, 149
  naming of, 29-30
  as party boat, 15, 16-17, 29-30, 45, 52-53, 125
  sailing, 18, 45, 125-34
  side decks, 107-8
  signed over to Bob Duncan, 17, 18, 47, 125
  winter layup, 47-48, 60

Eldredge, Captain Asa, 55

engine, 49, 50-58
  controls/instrument panel, 165-66
  diesel vs. gas, 50, 57
  docking and anchoring without, 50-55, 128-29
  Universal Atomic 4 (gas), 49, 57
  Yanmar (diesel), 49, 58

Englishman Bay, 19, 54

*Enterprise*, USS, 158

Evans, Jill, 103

**F**

fastenings, silicon-bronze, 35

fiberglass boats, 43, 68

fittings and hardware, 87-88, 120-122, 165-66, 177-79, 185-87

float, rigging and launching, 122-23, 172-73, 191-92

floor timbers, 108-109, 111

*Flying Scud*, 161

fog:
  motoring in, 56
  sailing in, 38-40, 38-39, 53, 54, 157-58

fore hatch, 110, 138, 141, 196

frames:
  bending in, 90-95

dubbing (fairing), 97-98
Frenchman Bay, 56-57
Friendship sloop, 32
see also *Eastward*; *Hieronymus*;
   *Tannis*; *Venture*
Friendship Sloop Society, 22,
   107, 113

**G**
gaff jaws, 59, 149, 169-71,
   173
gaff rig, 23, 50
*Georgie C. Bowden* (sloop), 55
Gloucester fishing schooners,
   24, 31-32, 33-34, 55, 66,
   158
Grand Manan Island, 157-58
Guild, Captain Boyd, 55

**H**
*Halifax*, wreck of, 19
Head of the Charles Regatta,
   45, 47, 48
Herreshoff H-28 (ketch), 18,
   20
Herreshoff Rozinante
   (ketch), 17-18, 30, 32
*Hieronymus* (Friendship
   sloop), 68
Hodgdon, Tim, 148

**I**
Ireland, Brad and Barbara,
   136
Islesboro, 64-65

**J**
Jenness, Charlie, 143, 146

Jinny, sailmaker, 151-54
Johnson, Irving, 158
Jonathan, boatbuilder, 92, 99,
   105
Jones, Tristan, 136-37

**K**
ketch, 17-18, 21, 29, 30-31,
   32
   sailing, 30-31, 32
   vs. schooner, 21, 30, 34
knees, grown, 59-60, 149

**L**
lee shore, 41
   anchoring on, 196
   motoring away from, 56-57
lobster boat construction
   (fisherman style), 27, 35,
   44, 93-94
lofting, 15, 67, 69-71
Longfellow, Henry
   Wadsworth, 42, 43
Luke, Frank, 60-62, 172,
   175, 181, 185, 187-89, 192
   see also Luke, Paul E., Inc.
Luke, John, 49, 63, 66, 184
Luke, Paul, 60-61
Luke, Paul E., Inc., 60-62,
   137-38, 206
   anchor, 61-62
   cabin heater, 61
   feathering propellers, 61
Lunenburg Foundry, 66

**M**
Maine:
   end of summer, 147-48

Vacationland, 171-72
Maine Boatbuilders Show, 87, 120
Marsh, Jon, 183
mast hoops, 87, 196
masts:
 rigging, 175-77, 180-81
 spruce, filling checks in, 139-40, 175-76
 stepping, 184, 187-88
Matinicus Harbor, 55
McFarland, Captain Ed, 27, 191
McFarland, Captain Riley, 191
McIntyre, Fred, 137
Menemsha Harbor, 110
Miner, Peggy, 193
mooring, shooting, 131, 133-34
Morse, Wilbur, 98
Mott, Greg, 165-66
Mott's Marine Salvage, 165-66
Mount Desert Island, 89
 *see also* Bar Harbor; Northeast Harbor; Southwest Harbor
Muscle Ridge Channel, 18, 53-54

**N**
naming a boat, 28-30
Narragansett Bay, 65
natural crooks, 59-60, 149
navigation, 157-63
 dead reckoning, 162
navigation instruments

chip log, 162
compass, 157-61
electronics, 87, 162-63, 185
knotmeter, 162, 185
ship's clock, 161-62
New Harbor, 27, 55, 137, 191
Newman, Jarvis, 68
*Niliraga* (centerboard schooner), 33, 35, 68
Northeast Harbor, 19-20

**O**
oak, gray (Maine-grown red oak), 35, 71

**P**
Page, Bill, 174, 177-79
Peer, Gerry, 187
Penobscot Bay, 54
Perry, Rich, 165-66
Pert Lowell, 87
planking, 96-105
 cedar for, 35, 40
 fairing (dubbing) frames for, 97-98
 garboard plank, 97-102
 shutter plank, 103
 spiling, 97, 99, 102
Pleasant Point Gut, St. George River, 178
Porcupine Islands, 56-57
portlights, 120-22

**R**
*Red Jacket* (clipper ship), 55
rope, nylon, splicing, 122
Royall, Keith, 172, 187-88

running lights, 178-79
running rigging
  belaying pins, 66
  blocks, 66, 178, 183-84
  parrel beads, 66
  pinrails and belaying pins,
   189
  sheets, travelers, cleats,
   and fairleads, 165, 197-99
  sway hooks, 185-87, 195

**S**

sail, docking under, 50-53,
  55, 128, 129
sailcloth, 155
  Oceanus, 142, 151, 156
sails, 49, 63-64, 142, 151-54,
  189-90
  *see also* schooner
sails, shortening, 30-31, 38
  on ketch, 30-31, 32
  on schooner, 31, 34
schooner, 21-22, **29**, 31-32,
  33-34
  bowsprit, 34, 36
  double head rig, 34-35, 46,
   48
  gaff main topsail, 46, 48,
   151
  Gloucester fisherman, 24,
   31-32, 33-34, 55, 66, 158
  jib, roll-up, 34, 46, 189-90,
   192, 198-99
  vs. ketch, 21, 30, 34
  main topsail, 46, 48, 151
  sailing, 31, 34, 196-205,
   207-9
  shoal-draft, 21-22, 30, 31
  standing rigging for,

   166-69, 175-77, 180-81
  staysail, 46
  *see also Dorothy Elizabeth*
Seal Cove, Grand Manan
  Island, 157
seamanship
  docking and anchoring
   under sail, 50-53, 55,
   128, 129, 196
  independence and
   self-reliance, 16, 39-40,
   191-92
Sharp, Captain, 55
Sherman, Tim, 149
Simmons, Brad, 136
sloop, **29**, 31, 51-52
  *see also Dorothy (sloop)*;
   *Eastward*
Smith, Captain Herb, 199
Southwest Harbor, 51, 55
*see also* Stanley, Ralph
spars, 49, 63, 139
  boom jaws, 173
  gaff jaws, 59, 149-50,
   169-71, 173
  rigging the masts, 175-77,
   180-81
  spruce, checks in, 139-40,
   175-76
  stepping the masts, 184,
   187-88
  topmast, 184
standing rigging, for
  schooner, 166-69
  rigging the mast, 175-77,
   180-81
  splicing wire, 77-86, 102,
   135, 166-68
  galvanic corrosion, 86

swaged terminal fittings,
86, 198
*see also* wire rigging,
splicing
Stanley, Marion, 22-23,
193, 201-2
Stanley, Ralph, 11-12, 20,
90-93, 97-98, 102, 105,
193, 201-2, 206
on bending in frames,
93-95
career of, 12, 68
clipper-bowed schooner,
21-22
design of *Dorothy
Elizabeth*, 21-25, 27-28,
32-35
on design of *Dorothy
Elizabeth*, 32-35
Friendship sloops, 68
historian, 22, 88-90
on ketch rig, 21, 32
lobster boats, 23-24, 27,
35, 42, 68, 93-94
on Roger's aneurysm,
114-15
on schooner rig, 32-34
on wooden boat building,
41-43
Stanley, Ralph, boat shop of,
20-21, 36-37, 88-95,
96-105
Stanley, Richard, 20, 69,
71-73, 90-93, 97-101,
104-5, 119-20, 140,
143-44
staysail, 46, 51-52
backing, 55
steering, 64-66
tiller, 64-65
vessel sailing herself, 65
worm gear system, 65-66
sway hooks, 185-87, 198
Swift (Rozinante ketch),
17-18, 30

**T**
Tannis (Friendship sloop),
173
thunder squall, 40. 130-34
Toss, Brion, *The Rigger's
Apprentice*, 168-69
Traditional Marine
Outfitters, 87-88, 120-22
Turnabout, 122, 155

**V**
Vaughan, Hal, 191
Venture (Friendship sloop),
68

**W**
waterline, marking, 140
White, Ridge, 158
Williams, Hugh, 50-51, 137,
202-4, 208
Wilson, Nathaniel S.,
sailmaker, 49, 63-64, 142,
153-56, 168, 192, 206
wire rigging, splicing, 77-86,
102, 135, 166-68
marlinespike work, 79-82
parceling and serving,
82-85, 169
skills and training, 77-79
vs. swaged terminal
fittings, 86
wire straps, 166-69

*see also* standing rigging
wooden boat:
  asset to community, 38,
    206-7
  beauty, 35, 41
  launching, 42
  market/demand for, 137
  uniqueness and aliveness,
    40, 42, 128, 207
*see also* boat
wooden boat, building,
  36-38, 40-43
  finishing off a bare hull,
    16, 28, 48, 191-92
  vs. fiberglass, 43
  fisherman style, 27, 35,
    44

skills and training, 21,
  36-37, 41, 43, 68, 69
wooden boat, rigging and
  maintaining:
self-reliance, 16, 191-92
wooden boat shop
  asset to community, 37-38,
    42-43
  fire, 94-95
  zoning, 42-43
  *see also* Stanley, Ralph,
    boat shop of
Woolcott, Travis and John,
  184

**Y**
yawl, **29**, 65, 110